Emerging Worship

Creating Worship Gatherings for New Generations

Dan Kimball

ZONDERVAN®

GRAND RAPIDS, MICHIGAN 49530

ZONDERVAN.COM/
AUTHORTRACKER

To all those who have felt restless and dared to think differently about the emerging church and emerging worship. You are not crazy and you are not alone.

ZONDERVAN®

Emerging Worship: Creating New Worship Gatherings for Emerging Generations
Copyright © 2004 by Dan Kimball

Requests for information should be addressed to:
Zondervan, Grand Rapids, Michigan 49530

Edited by David Sanford
Cover design by Mark Arnold
Interior design by Jon Arnold

Printed in the United States of America

08 09 10 • 15 14 13

Contents

Part 1

Part 2

Additional Chapters Online

Visit www.vintagefaith.com to read two additional chapters to this book:

A Personal Plea to Senior Pastors

A Personal Plea to Emerging Leaders Starting New Worship Gatherings

A Foreword by David Crowder

As is often typical of the custom of writing books, what follows is known as a foreword. Traditionally it's a collection of words written by some person or persons of knowledge regarding the contents contained within the book you perhaps found yourself holding in your hands, but I feel compelled to share with you the following:

fore·word   (fôr w rd, f r -)

n.

A preface or an introductory note, as for a book, especially by a person other than the author.

Source: *The American Heritage® Dictionary of the English Language,* Fourth Edition Copyright © 2000 by Houghton Mifflin Company. Published by Houghton Mifflin Company. All rights reserved.

As you readily see, there is, in fact, no necessary clause demanding knowledge of any kind to write a foreword. And so I find myself here with you now. Granted, I have led worship in Dan Kimball's church on a number of occasions and have felt his words and observed his people. And it is true that I am on staff at a church consisting of mostly college-aged congregants. And my official title there is Music and Arts Pastor, which sounds very important and useful when writing words preceding a book of this nature. But I must confess I don't feel very confident at this moment. No, I confess now that leading a community of people with the task of connecting them to the story of God is actually a terrifying thing to me. And while it is also true that I spend most of my weekdays somewhere in America leading roomfuls of people in corporate worship, I'm left no less confused by the climate of our current church culture. Perhaps I feel the urgency of new ways to carry the story of God more acutely because of it.

All that to say, I need a book like this. This seems reason enough to have someone else (perhaps you, there, reading these words) offer a foreword regarding the contents herein. But I shall again refer you to the requirements as defined by *The American Heritage® Dictionary of the English Language,* Fourth Edition Copyright ©2000 by Houghton Mifflin Company. It seems the only requirement is that I'm not the author of this book. That, it seems, is especially important. So, on an introductory note I'd like to say the following: This is a good book. It has a good weight to it. It feels good to hold in the hands or tuck in a bag. It also looks good on your shelf. When others see it there, they will think you informed and a constant student. The words inside settle in your soul well. They bang around in there until something's different, back where it belongs or set back upright like it should be. It smells good. It has that good book scent to it. You will laugh. Out loud. I think there will be some of you who are sad, and you will be moved to tears and want things to be different. You will help make them so. There are stories inside this book. Remember the feeling of cotton candy at the fair? You will want more, but your stomach will ache. You should use prudence. Remember elementary school pictures? The photographer always called me String Bean. (How did he remember year after year? I cut my own hair before my second grade picture. I wore a Pittsburgh Steelers' jersey, and he called me String Bean.) This book will help you remember. Remembering will bring you joy and pain, and you will see how you cut your own hair and why it was not good. It will hurt to see what is wrong, but you will help make it better. You will. You can. And you will laugh. You will laugh out loud because we are not done yet. In fact this could be a beginning. This book might just be a start. Or maybe it comes in the middle. It rattles just the same. And if you're at the end, the very end, maybe it will take you back to the start? Did I mention it has a really nice smell? It does. So exhale and then as deeply as you are able, gently and with delicate approach, breathe it in.

David Crowder lives in Waco, Texas, with his wife, Toni, where he has a lot of books on his shelf in hopes of impressing his friends. He thinks himself a constant student. He helped start University Baptist Church and is still the music and arts pastor there. He is also a small part of the fabulous rock and roll extravagance known as David Crowder Band on the recording label Sixsteps/Sparrow Records. (He is writing this spiel in third person because that's just the way it's done in the custom of writing spiels.)

A Foreword by Sally Morgenthaler

When it comes to irony, worship in late twentieth century evangelicalism takes the prize. Just as the world was reenchanting the universe (think Deepak Chopra, *The X-Files*, candle-and-teddy-bear grief vigils, *Final Fantasy* video games, and *Lord of the Rings*), user-friendly Christianity was practicing religious reductionism: shrinking the divine to the size of a three-point outline and four songs in the key of perpetually happy. In denuded corporate temples across America—from strip-mall spaces bathed in eerie green fluorescent lighting to gaping grey warehouses adrift in theater seats—turn-of-the-millennium "trendy" church is proving anything but trendy in a highly spiritualized culture.

The disenchantment of God has been no accident. For the last 25 years, a whatever-works, felt-needs theology has all but obscured the Three-in-One, veiled-in-flesh God of the Grand Narrative. What we have left in the God-of-the-bare-grey-box is nothing less than baptized unitarianism—God Generic sprinkled with just enough Christianese to justify the pastor's seminary education, the congregation's fading denominational affiliation, or simply the word *church* on the marquis. Each Sunday—from sea to shining sea and service-to-not-so-shining service—God Generic is addressed in predictable and monotone nonspecificity via hundreds of subcultural praise choruses. What's worse, it is the mono-God gone utilitarian...the great Whatever on-call to make your life whatever you want it to be. If historic worship is first and foremost about God, then disenchanted worship is about human units in their individual padded seats. As a recent rental car commercial intones, "It's all about you." Worship of the disenchantment takes that phrase seriously.

Given its ever-increasing disconnect with the surrounding culture, it's also no accident that supposedly user-friendly Christianity is losing its youngest contingent. As a former youth pastor and now emerging church pastor, Dan Kimball has been charting the young and the restless' exit for well over a decade. In this crucial volume (sequel to *The Emerging*

Church), Dan gives voice to the emerging generations' mounting impatience with the interminable "80s worship movie." He also lends shape to their visions of fresh God-encounters. *What does it mean — this side of disenchantment — to engage with a God of mystery and paradox? A God Who is transcendent as well as imminent? What does it mean to craft worship collaboratively, to jettison top-down hierarchies, to move preaching from centerpiece to one among many pieces? What would it be like to radically repackage ancient forms? And what is worship anyway? Is it equivalent to music?* (Just so you know, Dan loves worship music. But don't expect to find a whole lot of discussion about it here. Dan's too busy exploring all the unused avenues of worship expression.) Dan also does a good job of deconstructing the trend-chaser church's fascination with worship technology. Does good worship depend on how many toys and tricks we have in the house, or might it require a foundation beyond the almighty power outlet?

In the final analysis, *Emerging Worship* is both unapologetic critique of worship-in-the-box (post-1980s and modern) and a practitioner's guidebook to worship-beyond-the-box (postmillennial and postmodern). "Oh, no!" you moan. "Another postmodern pontiff!" Don't worry. Dan Kimball's gracious, authentic spirit clearly disqualifies him as a condescending emerging church guru. You'll find no arrogance here. Only honest questions, honest stories, and honest dreams of God — and worship — reenchanted for the church's largest missing people group.

Sally Morgenthaler is author of Worship Evangelism: Inviting Unbelievers into the Presence of God, *a touchstone for postmodern, worship-driven ministry and a work whose popularity spans denominational boundaries. Founder of Sacramentis.com ("Re-imagining Worship for a New Millennium)," Sally's vision is to move worship beyond presentation (information, performed music, and preaching) to an interactive, sacred experience involving all the arts. She lives in Colorado with her two children.*

Acknowledgments

We are living in an interesting time as we pray, rethink, reimagine, and rediscover what it means to be the church and to be holistic worshipers and followers of Jesus Christ. We didn't ask to be in this sometimes confusing transitional period of the emerging church, but it is where Jesus seems to have placed us. The great news is that many of us are in this adventure together—sharing ideas, lessons, and thoughts as we go along.

I want to thank those who helped shape this book and contributed their ideas and experiences of emerging worship. Special thanks to Nancy Ortberg and Steve Gillen from Willow Creek Community Church, Andy Lewis and Rob Patterson from Twin Lakes Church, Jason Evans from Matthew's House, Brad Cecil from Axxess Fellowship, Jonny Baker and Steve Collins from Grace Church, London, and Ken Baugh and Denny Henderson from McLean Bible Church.

In my own local context, I want to thank Bonnie Wolf, Dave Gschwend, and Peter Wilkes for believing in the vision of Vintage Faith Church and helping it become reality through Santa Cruz Bible Church. Special thanks to my wife, Becky, to musical worship leader Josh Fox, and to all those in the Vintage Faith Church leadership community as we pursue our new mission together.

I want to thank David Sanford for all the work in editing this book. Also, Youth Specialties and Mark Oestreicher and the emergentYS board — Tony Jones, Brian McLaren, Doug Pagitt, Kara Powell, Jay Howver, and John Raymond — whom God has placed in a very strategic place to help shape the future emerging church.

INTRODUCTION

The Emerging Restlessness That Cannot Be Ignored

The way we traditionally expressed Christianity may be in trouble, but the future may hold new expressions of the Christian faith every bit as effective, faithful, meaningful, and world-transforming as those we've know so far.
—Brian McLaren

I grew up in the New York City suburb of Paramus, New Jersey. Land of Bruce Springsteen, Bon Jovi, and *The Sopranos.*

A very popular New Jersey suburban pet at the time was the French poodle. They came complete with decorative and carefully shaved puffs of poodle hair on their legs and at the end of their tail giving them their unique poodle look. We owned a silver gray poodle named Bel Ami. I know poodles have a reputation of being whiny, little, yapping, feminine-looking dogs. So before I tell the story, I need to give an apologetic for the poodle.

Most people have no idea about this, but poodles are actually considered one of the most intelligent breeds. Most people also don't realize that poodles were once popular and skillful hunting dogs in Europe and were known for their ability to retrieve waterfowl. You may think poodles are rather sissy-dogs, but in reality poodles are actually masculine warrior hunting dogs with extreme intelligence. (That's my poodle apologetic and I am proud to have been a poodle owner.)

Anyway, back in New Jersey my grandfather was a frequent visitor to our house. Our poodle really loved and had a special attachment to my grandfather. But what was fascinating was that our poodle had the uncanny ability to sense in advance when my grandfather was coming to our house.

I distinctly remember how our poodle sensed my grandfather coming over and would begin hanging out by the front door an hour or so before his arrival. He would begin to get restless and start pacing back and forth. He became more and more impatient the closer it got to my grandfather's actual arrival. You could see the dissatisfaction and restlessness growing. He would even jump up on a chair and peek out the window to see if my grandfather was coming. Sometimes, he let out a little bark or two in hopes that he could speed up my grandfather's arrival.

When my grandfather finally arrived, and the door was opened, our poodle became overjoyed. He would leap up to greet my grandfather. For the whole time he was at our house, our poodle would never leave his side.

Emerging Restlessness in the Church

My poodle had an instinctive awareness that someone was coming and was restless and pacing — waiting for him to arrive. In the same way, there is an instinctive awareness and restlessness growing among emerging church leaders and emerging generations. They are both waiting for change in the church to arrive. We don't know exactly when it all is going to fully arrive, but we instinctively sense it is coming.

Emerging leaders sense not only change coming to our churches, but the critical need for change. In many churches it has already arrived. The emerging leaders of those churches are beginning to reshape and rethink church and the Spirit of God is doing wonderful things. But there is still a growing restlessness in many hearts and minds. People are emotionally pacing back and forth waiting and longing for change in the church to finally arrive.

This restless emotional pacing is due to the way most of our churches do not connect and engage with our emerging post-Christian culture. The church engages with a modern culture — with those who have modern values and a Judeo-Christian worldview. But most people (especially emerging generations) are living in post-Judeo-Christian times now.

Lots of churches are packed primarily with people 35 years and older. In light of this, we can't assume everything is all hunky dory.

Where Are All the 18- to 35-Year-Olds?

Emerging generations are increasingly being born and raised with a different philosophical set of values, a changing worldview, and an evolving belief system that generations before them did not experience. This definitely impacts both disciples of Jesus as well as those who are unchurched.

Many churches are seeing fewer and fewer emerging generations in their communities because of this cultural shift. There is a rising murmur among pastors and leaders, "Where are all the 18- to 35-year-olds?" It goes beyond young adults, as there is also a noticeable trend that youth growing up outside of the church are not in our churches either. Yes, we still have younger people in church. Usually that is only because they either grew up in the church or transferred from another church.

It gets scary when you start looking at the percentages of teenagers in local communities who are not part of any church. This causes informed church leaders to emotionally pace back and forth. But it's not just emerging church leaders who are restless and pacing.

I'm Leaving My Church to Be a Disciple of Jesus

More and more emerging generations who were raised in the church are saying that there must be something more to "church" than what they have experienced. The systems we use to teach them how to be disciples of Jesus are not connecting with them like they did for generations past. Emerging generations say it just doesn't "feel right" or "fit right" anymore. They want to be disciples of Jesus, but how we approach disciple-making needs to shift right alongside their shifting values.

Emerging generations wonder if what they have been taught about "community" — and what they've seen promoted in their churches—is really biblical community at all.

They wonder if what they were taught about evangelism is really the right way to think about, and practice, sharing the gospel of Jesus. They are wondering if being a Christian and being "saved" is more than just saying a prayer to get to heaven. They are asking why the church doesn't talk more often about the Kingdom of God and why most Christians don't take interest in social justice.

They wonder why preaching has turned the beautiful and mysterious story of God and man into self-help guru Tony Robbins-like teaching with some Bible verses added. They wonder why their hunger to discover and wrestle with the deeper depths of Scripture is fed with neatly packaged versions of how-to messages and pat Bible-answers.

They are getting restless.

And they are pacing.

I've had numerous conversations with younger people who told me they left their church to be a disciple of Jesus in a way that makes sense to them. They aren't abandoning their faith. Many choose to form small faith communities and meet in homes among friends. They are waiting for the larger, more organized church to change. This is no cop-out, either.

Virtually every young adult I have talked to sincerely tried to bring change to their church and brought suggestions to their church leadership before leaving their church.

Most volunteered to start something new. But the suggestions fell on deaf ears with a predetermined view of what emerging generations should be like in relation to "church."

The closed minds in their church leadership eventually made them choose to leave.

Watching Reruns of a 1980s TV Show

I talked with a young mother who told me that she and her husband recently left their evangelical megachurch even though they didn't want to. She felt that in many ways she "outgrew" what her church offered her to participate in. She couldn't even put her finger on exactly what she was looking for. She said that being in her church's worship services was like watching a rerun of a 1980s TV show over and over again. The whole thing didn't speak to her anymore. It didn't challenge her because it felt so programmatic, constrictive, and limiting.

They were longing to express their worship to God when they came to church. But they felt restricted to passively sitting in their seats and worshiping as they were told. They longed for community, but the small group programs of the church felt so controlled and superficial. They didn't feel it was the true community they were looking for. They explored places to serve and be involved, but the primary ways were to keep the weekend 1980s TV show running. This was a very large church. They had tons going on but this couple felt more and more uneasy as time went on.

This couple tried hard not to leave their church! Time and time again, she lovingly and truly tried to express her feelings to the pastor. She offered suggestions and even volunteered to help out. When she shared, she received a mini-lecture about how all younger people go through times like she was. She was told to stop being so self-centered, to not complain about the worship service, and to remember that worship is about God — not her personal preferences.

This couple grew tired of pacing and left the church. They are now part of a small house church.

Emerging Restlessness with Worship Services

This rising disconnection of values and emotional pacing has a lot do with most churches' worship services. This book focuses on worship services and offers some ideas of how churches are changing to address this. Weekend worship services are becoming a definite issue for emerging generations. They wonder if coming together to worship really only consists of a few songs and a central focus on preaching. They feel more and more uncomfortable with the way many worship services profile one or two male-only leaders up front. They are wondering why there is hardly (if any at all) participation from the people in the congregation.

In terms of music, they feel more and more embarrassed by many of the lyrics in popular worship songs. Many feel unsettled by the way the song leader leads or the way the band plays. (When explored, you will find that these comments about music usually go way beyond generational music styles or personal preferences. It entirely has to do with values of what and how musical worship is done in a worship gathering. We will address this later).

They wonder why they can't have more freedom in worship to express to God their love and passion for him in ways that resonate with who they are. They wonder why they are seeing fewer and fewer people their own age. So, they are getting restless.

They are pacing while they wait for change to come—or at least for freedom to contribute and lead the way to change in their church.

Opening the Door to Welcome Change

We are at an interesting point for many of our churches. If you are observing the pacing and restlessness, it is time for you to begin opening the door.

My poodle knew my grandfather was coming and began pacing and getting restless. Eventually that door would swing open, and my grandfather would come in. We in church leadership have the opportunity to begin opening the door in our churches to allow change to come in.

You may not feel comfortable with change. Or you may not understand yet what it is that you will do. The important thing is that you desire emerging generations to truly connect with God and worship him in your worship services. This must be in a way that they can connect with God and slow down their restless pacing. Some churches are doing exciting things to "open the door." Several of them are profiled in this book — not to tell you what to do, but to inspire you to think through what the Spirit of God may or may not want to do in your church. Every church is different. There isn't only one way or one approach.

My personal hope and prayer is that you won't ignore the restlessness going on, but instead that:

- You will be concerned enough about the pacing and restlessness going on among emerging generations in your church to "open the door" and pray through the changes your church needs.

- You will be concerned enough about the lack of emerging generations in your church to pray, think, and rethink what your church can do to address it.

- Above all, that you will be open-minded. That you will not be too proud to recognize that our methodologies and forms of how we go about "doing church" do change throughout biblical and church history. That you will be open-minded to consider that what you may be doing now may not be what is needed to connect with the values and worldview of emerging generations. That you will be open-minded enough to explore the Scriptures to see what it says about "church" and about "worship" and worship gatherings. That you will use those Scripture as a framework rather than what you were taught from your past church experiences, from seminary, or even from this book!

The Great Joy of Opening the Door to Change

When I see the responses within churches willing to rethink what they do, especially in their worship services, I have great joy and hope. I've heard beautiful stories of churches that have a passion for emerging generations. They are taking pioneering steps to allow change in the door. These stories are about churches rethinking "church." Because of their insights, they are leveraging what is going on in our post-Christian culture with such joyful responses and results. Worship services are now happening all around the country, and there emerging generations are connecting with and worshiping God.

This book focuses on the worship gatherings themselves. It tells the story of churches who are creating, or have created, gatherings that connect with the emerging culture. Before we get into the actual services, however, we need to look at a few critical things.

A Few Reminders

As we investigate emerging worship services, we cannot look at them as if we were merely designing a program or school play. Our goal is to create a gathering where the holy God who created the universe and everything in it will be worshiped (Philippians 2:10-11). We are creating a time for the saints to gather and encourage one another (Hebrews 10:25), a gathering where unbelievers joining us will know without a doubt that God is among us (1 Corinthians 14:25).

Let's start by taking a closer look at what emerging worship is, in the hope that we will then know how to craft effective worship gatherings.

Emerging Thoughts

1. Can you relate to the description of the restlessness growing among emerging generations regarding church and worship services? If so, in what ways?

2. What are some specific examples of things in your church service that may cause emerging generations to feel disconnected?

Ongoing Discussion and Examples of Emerging Worship

Visit www.vintagefaith.com for articles about the emerging church and emerging worship. This Web site also features examples and photographs from various emerging worship gatherings.

Peter and Joyce Majendie

CHAPTER 1

What is an emerging worship ~~service~~ gathering?

Come, let us bow down in worship,
let us kneel before the LORD our Maker.
—Psalm 95:6

Worship is certainly a popular word these days. There are now several major "worship" conferences every year. Now that it is easier to locally record and duplicate CDs, many churches and youth groups are putting out their own worship CDs. Stacks of "Best of Worship" compilation CDs are promoted on late night television stations. Many popular Christian musicians — who normally never recorded worship songs — now have come out with "worship" CDs of their own. Even John Tesh, former co-host of *Entertainment Tonight*, has put out his own worship CDs.

Worship has been quite the rage lately. But what is "worship" and what is a "worship gathering"? These are critical questions to ask before we even think of discussing creating emerging worship gatherings.

Emerging Worship Is Not Just Singing

This book is titled *Emerging Worship: Creating New Worship Gatherings for Emerging Generations*. It is all about creating worship gatherings where new generations come to worship. But what does "worship" look like?

I believe to the average person, and even to most pastors, music is what primarily comes to mind. In fact, in many churches worship pastors lead the singing portion of the worship service. Like me, you've probably heard individuals say with great passion, "I love to worship!" Almost every time, they are talking about singing.

As you read this book, you will find it has little to do with singing and music. Like many others, I desire to see worship — and worship gatherings — change from primarily singing to something a lot more holistic and a lot more biblical.

Emerging Worship Is Not a Worship Service

We usually call the weekend time when a church family gets together a "worship service." Ironically, this term used to mean a time when the saints of God all meet to offer their service to God through worship and their service to others in the church. Over time, however, the title has slowly reversed. The weekend worship "service" has become the time of the week when we go to a church building much like a car goes to an automobile service station.

Most people view the weekend worship service as a place where we go to get service done to us by "getting our tanks filled up" at the service station. It's a place where someone will give a sermon and serve us with our weekly sustenance. In automobile terms, you could say it is our weekly fill-up. We come to our service station to have a song leader serve us by leading us in singing songs. All so we can feel good when we emotionally connect through mass singing and feel secure that we did "worship."

We go to the weekend worship service and drop off our kids — that way they too can get served by having their weekly fill-ups. We are especially glad that our weekend service station now serves coffee in the church lobby — it's as convenient as our automobile service station's little mini-mart.

Not a Local Automotive Station

I admit that I'm being somewhat sarcastic with the service station analogy. But I'm not joking when I say we need to recognize that going to a worship service is not about us, the worshipers. It is not about God's service to us. It is purely our offering of service and worship to God — offering our lives, offering our prayers, offering our praise, offering our confessions, offering our finances, offering our service to others in the church body.

The description of a church gathering in 1 Corinthians 14: 26-27 says: "What then shall we say, brothers? When you come together, everyone has a hymn, or a word of instruction, a revelation, a tongue or an interpretation. All of these must be done for the strengthening of the church."

This was not "come together to sit and receive" like at a gas station. This was everyone gathering to offer service to God and others in worship. The gathering was not primarily about meeting the needs of the individual, but centered on the worship of God and the strengthening of the whole church.

In the New Testament, the English word "service" (as translated in the New International Version) is used to speak of an act of giving, not receiving. Paul spoke of his ministry by saying, "Therefore I glory in Christ Jesus in my service to God" (Romans 15:17). Paul talked quite frequently about his "service" to the saints, which meant Paul was serving them.

Nevertheless, the "worship service," where the focus is supposed to be us bringing our services to God by worshiping him, has been subtly changed to focus more on us getting served by going to the meeting.

Because of the subtle misuse of the phrase "worship service," I don't use it anymore. I try to always say "worship gathering" instead. Theologically, this communicates what we are doing much better. Once again we can be the church gathering to worship God and bring our service and offerings to him and others, not individuals who come to a service to receive something. There is a big, big difference in people's expectations between the two ways of looking at what we do when we meet together for worship.

So, the more we in leadership can communicate that this is a worship gathering (not a worship service), the more it will shift people's expectations of what the goal is when we meet together.

Emphasizing "worship gatherings" is vital for the emerging church.

Emerging Worship as a Lifestyle

Worship is "the act of adoring and praising God, that is, ascribing worth to God as the one who deserves homage and service." The most frequent Greek New Testament word for worship is *proskuneo* which stems from *pros* ("toward") and *kuneo* ("to kiss"). This is an act of reverence and devotion, and in biblical times often involved bowing, kneeling, and lying prostrate in reverence before a great and holy God. Worship is the way to express our love and praise to Jesus, who first loved us and gave himself up for us (Ephesians 5:25).

In a worship gathering, we create a place where we can express love, devotion, adoration, and praise to God. This should shape our planning and design. But worship is not something we do only once a week on Sunday morning or evening. Worship is a lifestyle of being in love with God and in awe of him all week long (Romans 12:1-2). It is offering our love, our adoration, and our praise to him through all of our lives.

We are to adore the Lord all week, not just at "worship gatherings." Our minds, our hearts, our bodies, our marriages, our families, our jobs — everything should be offered to him in worship. This includes what we think about, what we do, what we say, what we eat, and what we spend time doing — they are all acts of worship.

It is so important to make sure we know worship is a lifestyle and those in our

"Jesus was born of a virgin, suffered under Pontius Pilate, died on the cross and rose from the dead to make worshipers out of rebels!"
—A. W. Tozer

churches also know it! How extremely sad that we have trained people to think that worship primarily happens when they come to church and sing.

It is my hope that the emerging church will be extremely careful to embrace and teach a biblical view of true worship.

Reclaiming a Holistic Form of Worship

This book is specifically about emerging worship gatherings. Our focus will be on exploring different ways that emerging generations are now coming together to adore, praise, and ascribe worth to God.. A refreshing thing is that — virtually across the board — we are moving away from a flat, two-dimensional form of worship in our gatherings. There is a definite move away from worship services simply composed of preaching and a few songs. We are now moving toward a much more multisensory approach comprised of many dimensions and expressions of worship.

We now see art being brought into worship, the use of visuals, the practice of ancient disciplines, the design of the gathering being more participatory than passive-spectator. Instead of the pulpit and sermon being the central focus of worship gatherings (at least in most evangelical churches), we now see Jesus as the central focus through a variety of creative worship expressions. True, every preacher says that Jesus is the center of their preaching! What I mean here is that teaching and learning in the emerging church happen in various ways; it's no longer only one person standing on a stage preaching to everyone else.

I realize some people's blood pressure may begin to rise as soon as I mention moving away from a preaching-and-singing-a-few-songs worship service model to a multi-sensory approach to worshiping God. Someone actually told me that younger people only need preaching verse-by-verse through the Bible. He insisted that anything else is distracting and useless. Some individuals have warned me that emerging churches are going all experiential and throwing out God's Word. Other individuals have leveled the criticism that emerging churches are wrongly changing the historical way the Church has worshiped.

> "You alone are the LORD. You made the heavens, even the highest heavens, and all their starry host, the earth and all that is on it, the seas and all that is in them. You give life to everything, and the multitudes of heaven worship You."
> —Nehemiah 9:6

When I hear these types of comments, I question whether that person has truly ever studied church history. I wonder if they have ever looked in the Bible at the various ways worship gatherings happened. I know I might have felt the same thing they do — if I had never begun taking a biblical and historical look at worship through the ages.

Embracing the Historical Diversity of Worship

For the longest time, I assumed that the only biblically sound worship gathering was the tradition I had experienced in my evangelical, conservative church: a few songs, the sermon, a closing song, and communion thrown in once a month.

As I studied church history and the history of worship, however, I was amazed. The way I had personally experienced and defined a worship gathering was by no means what has been happening throughout the history of the church and the history of Christian worship.

It is critical for emerging church leaders to take the time to step outside of our personal or denominational view of what "church" and "worship gatherings" are supposed to be. When we back out and begin to open our eyes to other denominational approaches to worship and differing global approaches to worship, we will find so much beauty in the diversity of ways that people worship God.

I highly encourage church leaders to study and explore the history of worship. I highly encourage church leaders to ask why you even do the things you currently do in your worship gatherings. You may be surprised to discover that many things you do are forms of your denomination's origin culture and not from the Scriptures themselves.

It will be interesting in heaven because worship there probably won't be the worship we are used to in our local church! I think it is important to realize this, so we won't judge other churches who worship differently than we do. There is more than one way to worship God in a church gathering. We need to recognize and celebrate that! In fact, many forms of worship emerged throughout biblical history.

Emerging Worship Is Not New

It is important to understand that emerging worship is not simply "the new thing," nor is it simply the "hip, new way to worship." As we read the grand story of the Bible, we see that culture and time have changed worship throughout history. Various forms of worship have emerged throughout the story of God and man. Until Jesus returns, we will see many new expressions and forms of worship change in churches within various cultures.

The Bible repeatedly talks about new emerging forms of worship. This cannot be considered "trendy." We are simply part of another time period undergoing change in how emerging generations ascribe worth and praise to God. This type of change has been happened over and over throughout history.

In Genesis 4, Abel gave God fat portions from the firstborn of his flock and Cain gave God some of the fruits of the soil. Although Cain's worship was not pure, we see these brothers already had an established form of worship.

In Genesis 8:20, we see Noah worship by building an altar and sacrificing burnt offerings. These offerings were different from the sacrifices that Cain and Abel offered. Another form of worship emerged right after the flood.

In Genesis 13:18, Abraham built an altar to the Lord as an act of worship. He created a sacred space and used memorial props as a form of emerging worship.

In Genesis 28:22, we see another form of emerging worship. Jacob took a stone and set it up as a pillar. He poured oil on top of it and called the stone "God's house."

In different time periods throughout the Bible, all types of sacred spaces and structures have emerged for worship. The tabernacle was designed as a sacred space of worship. It had several courts with furnishings used for worship, including the ark, the table of showbread, and the lamp stand. It also had an altar for animal sacrifices. This place of worship was movable and traveled with the people.

The temple in Jerusalem was built many centuries later. This ushered in even more advanced and elaborate worship. The temple itself only dimly reflected the real heavenly dwelling (Hebrews 8:5), but again a new worship pattern was emerging.

In Malachi 1:10-11, we read about how worship emerged not just in the Temple in Jerusalem, but everywhere, with incense and pure offerings brought to God. The paradigm of worship shifts again!

The New Testament is full of emerging worship. Jesus shook up everything! He taught that worship is not attached to a location or space. Instead, true worship is done in spirit and truth (John 4:23-24). Jesus taught that God does not look for specific acts or rituals of worship. The heart behind the worship matters most to him.

Immediately after Jesus' ascension a new form of worship was birthed when the Spirit indwelled believers (Acts 2). The Spirit was no longer in the physical sacred space of the temple, but in believers. Our bodies became the temple where the Spirit dwells (1 Corinthians 6:19). Our entire lives are now spiritual acts of worship (Romans 12:1-2). We don't go to a certain place — we worship God with all we do!

The practice of gathering at the temple for rituals and complex sacrifices moved to the simplicity of gathering in people's homes (1 Corinthians 16:19, Colossians 4:15, Philemon 2). Each church gathered to share a meal, sing, read Scripture, and pray. The New Testament "worship service" (worship gathering) became very simplistic. There were no pulpits, no 45-minute four-point sermons, no worship bands, no ushers. Instead, everyone was prepared to participate. They set aside time for singing, teaching, discussion, and the Lord's Supper (1 Corinthians 11:17-34). They also gave each other a holy kiss (1 Corinthians 16:20).

As the church developed and grew and the surrounding culture influenced worship over the next few centuries, the church moved from meeting in homes to larger buildings based on the architecture of the Roman Basilica (the law court). Pews were brought in along with pulpits and choirs. These elements were already common to the Roman and Greek cultures and the pagan religions of that time period.

After a while, Christian worship gatherings took on more form through liturgy. Then other new forms of worship emerged within the ancient Catholic Church, the

Orthodox Church, and various monastic orders.

The buildings in which various churches gathered changed to reflect new cultural influences. Cathedrals, stained glass windows, and hymnals were all forms of emerging worship at one time.

In recent times, church architecture has changed again. We now have theater-like, multipurpose worship buildings, video screens, and many other innovations. But we haven't seen anything yet! The book of Revelation contains fantastic images of worship that will emerge in the future. They are beyond our grasp to comprehend now. But we see images that "God and the Lamb will be in the city and His servants will serve Him" (Revelation 22:3). There will be a day where we literally see and worship Jesus face to face!

So, as our current culture moves from a modern to postmodern world, it is only natural that new forms of worship are arising. Biblically and historically, it should come as no surprise that emerging generations feel a widespread sense of dissatisfaction with modern forms of Christian worship. We shouldn't be threatened by it, nor should we condemn forms of worship that don't feel comfortable to us. It doesn't mean previous forms of worship are invalid; just that new expressions are emerging — and will continue to emerge.

New Wineskins for Emerging Worship

In emerging churches, we desire new wineskins in our formal times of gathering for worship. Not in worship itself, nor in the act of worship (which is a lifestyle and therefore timeless), but in the shape of what our worship gatherings look and feel like. Jesus used a metaphor of new wineskins to describe the different approaches to God that he introduced.

The emerging church desires new wineskins for worship. These new wineskins are needed in response to our new postmodern culture. It is a terrible mistake to ignore this, and a somewhat arrogant one if we still believe that how we currently worship is the one and only way to worship God. I am not talking about worshiping a different God, after all! I'm only talking about worshiping God differently.

"Where is the one who has been born king of the Jews? We saw His star in the east and have come to worship Him." —Matthew 2:2

Taking Worship Seriously

One day, I believe that we will have to give account to Jesus for how we shepherded people in our churches (Hebrews 13:17) and how we led them in worship. When we meet Jesus and give an account to him for what we did in worship gatherings, I don't think he is going to be interested in what cool and nifty ways we came up with to worship him. I think he will be more interested in the prayerful times we spent designing a worship gathering. I think he will be more interested in what type of disciples our churches produced. I think he will be more interested in the hearts of the people who attended our worship gatherings than what we did in them. We had better be praying and thinking through what is most important in all of this discussion about worship. We better be asking the right questions.

Asking the Right Questions When Designing a Worship Gathering

The New Testament doesn't give a lot of information about what worship gatherings in the early church were like. But we do know enough — no matter what form our worship takes — to ask these questions:

1. Did we lift the name of Jesus up as the centerpiece of why we gathered? (See Revelation 5:6 and 5:13-14, Colossians 3:17, and Philippians 2:9-11.)
2. Did we have a time in the Scriptures learning the story of God and man? Did we invite everyone to be part of his story today in Kingdom living? (See 2 Timothy 3:14—4:4.)
3. Did we pray together and have enough time to slow down and quiet our hearts to hear God's voice and yield to his Spirit? (See Acts 1:14 and John 4:23-24.)
4. Did we experience the joy, love, and encouragement of being together as a church? (See Hebrews 10:25 and John 13:34-35.)
5. Did we take the Lord's Supper together as a church regularly? (See 1 Corinthians 11:20-32.)
6. Did we somehow remind everyone of the mission of the church and why we exist? (See Matthew 28:18-20.)
7. Did we enable people to individually contribute something as part of the body of Christ? (See 1 Corinthians 12:27 and 14:26.)

I wonder how often these questions are asked by leaders as we prepare for a worship gathering? Or do we usually focus more on questions such as "What songs should we sing this Sunday?" and "What announcements should we make?"

When we evaluate our worship gatherings afterward, do we ask the questions listed above, or do we ask "How good was the band?" and "How did the transition between the drama and the sermon go?" I know these things are important! But in the emerging church we must look at our worship gatherings, ask these questions first, and then design our worship gatherings with new priorities.

Worship gatherings are about the saints gathering to live out Psalm 95:6, which says, "Come, let us bow down in worship, let us kneel before the LORD our Maker." It is a multisensory approach of bowing, kneeling, listening, learning, looking, singing, caring, touching, and loving with our minds, our hearts, and our bodies. It is about seeing the results of worship, which produce in us a greater love for God and a greater love for people (Matthew 22:37-39). God forbid that we teach the people in our churches to view emerging worship as anything less.

Emerging Thoughts

1. Think about the difference between a "worship gathering" and a "worship service." In your particular church context, what is the difference between these two ways of looking at what we do each Sunday?

2. What would the people of your church say are the reasons your worship gathering exists?

CHAPTER 2

The paradox of creating alternative worship gatherings

Leave these men alone!
Let them go! For if their purpose or activity is of human origin,
it will fail. But if it is from God, you will not be able to stop
these men; you will only find yourself fighting against God.
— Acts 5:38-39

One of my favorite bands is the Ramones. The Ramones were birthed in many ways quite by accident. They were four teenage misfits from Queens, New York, who felt they could not relate with much of the music happening in the mid-1970s. Disco was rising in popularity, big arena commercial rock bands were popular, and there was John Denver and more Olivia Newton-John soft pop. Somehow, they knew in their gut that the music world needed to change. So they decided to start a band. They didn't even know how to play instruments. It wasn't until after they formed the band that the guitarist bought his first guitar.

The owner of the club where the Ramones first played said they were dumb for trying this new form of music. He was sure no one would like them. He was wrong. Soon they found that a lot of other people were also not resonating with the current music scene; they too knew that music needed some reinventing. At first, there were only a few such people. Millions were still totally happy to listen to the soft pop, disco, or arena rock music. But a slow, underground, growing number of people felt unsettled with the state of music at the time and began following the Ramones. In time, there was an entire legion of Ramones fans. But the Ramones did not pioneer this new genre of music easily. They experienced great struggle, tremendous criticism, and even mockery. They pioneered something new. There was no preset or prescribed way for designing and creating a new form of music. The Ramones were not known for being great musicians or songwriters. But they didn't give up on what they believed in.

After Joey Ramone died of cancer in 2001, Bono of U2 presented the remaining Ramones with a special award at the MTV Music Awards. Bono said that without the Ramones, there would be no U2. Bono credited the Ramones for influencing them to the point of inspiring U2's birth and existence as a band. Because the Ramones pioneered change, millions and millions of U2 fans now listen to what most of us would consider great music.

I am fully aware that you cannot equate the Ramones and the creation of punk music to the creation of worship services. In fact, the Ramones were a rather pagan band that by no means held to Christian ethics or morals. I am not endorsing their personal lifestyles, nor saying God was behind the birth of their music!

What I am trying to express are the principles behind a band that had enough passion about something they believed in to take risks, struggle to be understood, and go against the grain. We must remember this did not come easy for the Ramones. As I sit here writing this book about experimenting with emerging forms of worship and birthing new types of alternative worship gatherings for emerging generations, I too am feeling a great struggle.

Half of me would like to shout: "This is great! What a wonderful way to see churches engage the emerging culture and create gatherings that resonate with the hearts of post-Christian generations. What a fantastic way to grow the local body of Christ! We must do something, because what's at stake are emerging generations who have not yet experienced Jesus."

At the same time, the other half of me wants to yell: "Don't do it! It is tremendously hard work. If you are doing this in an existing church, you most likely will face incredible tension with church staff who won't understand what you are doing. It is a disaster in the making! You could lose your job over this. Stop before it's too late!"

The Agony and the Ecstasy

I have experienced the joy of seeing people come to know Jesus Christ because people rethought church and created an alternative worship gathering and ministry. I have seen the vision and dream of starting something new birthed until it grew to hundreds and hundreds of people worshiping Jesus with great joy. They were on their knees and faces praying and repenting. Their lives were totally changed.

I have seen churches in which a new alternative worship gathering brings fresh life and momentum to churches that before had been slowly dying. I have spoken with many pastors who are incredibly enthused about what God is doing in their churches — all because of they started new worship gatherings designed for a post-Christian culture.

I have had the privilege of talking at length with a youth pastor who wanted to start an alternative type of worship gathering and ministry in his church. Four years later, I saw more than 1,000 young believers praising God together at the service he had started. About a dozen were baptized the night I was there!

I have also heard of horribly sad stories and great struggles.

I have sat and prayed with a pastor who was fired from his church for starting an alternative service. The senior pastor got freaked out by some of the things they were doing. I recently received a sad e-mail from another pastor. He had actually brought his team and senior pastor to our church where we met and walked through ideas. They launched a new form of ministry and a new worship gathering. In a year, they had more than a hundred

> "This is what the LORD says: Let my people go, so that they may worship Me."
> —Exodus 8:1

people attending the alternative worship service. But then, with no warning, the senior pastor decided to shut it down. He wanted to send the people attending the alternative service to the main service where he preached because he thought that they needed to move into a "real" church service.

I ache every time I hear painful, hurtful, dream-squashing stories from those who ventured to try something different in their churches.

I too experienced frustration, misunderstanding, and tension when I started a new worship gathering and ministry in our church. That is why I struggle writing this. When you start to truly engage and resonate with post-Christian generations, it means rethinking worship. It means not being afraid to rethink church. Rethinking church is inevitable when you truly pioneer something instead of just changing outward appearances.

I understand that for some people, this type of rethinking is extremely difficult. Anyone used to doing ministry — and thinking of church and worship services — in a modern way will find it hard to grasp new ways to engage a postmodern culture.

Most of what we do in the emerging church doesn't fit in the old categories! There is no prescribed way to do this. There are no preset models to follow. The reality is that thinking through new approaches to ministry, starting new forms of worship gatherings, and fitting them within an existing church can lead to power and control struggles as well as disagreements, heartache, pain, and tension.

But don't give up — it is worth it!

The Payoff for Making It through the Good, the Bad, and the Ugly

Every time I struggle with the paradox of creating alternative worship gatherings, I come back to the fact that we must take risks to see these changes happen in our churches. Too much is at stake not to try to start new worship gatherings and ministries in our churches. Otherwise, how will emerging post-Christian generations, who have grown up completely outside of the modern church, come to faith in Jesus Christ?

Pastor Bill Hybels, in a Willow Creek Defining Moments message, commented on whether a church should start a new alternative worship service and ministry for emerging generations. He said:

What I keep coming back to is that the alternative [of not starting a new worship service and ministry] is unthinkable. For anybody to sit idly by and watch one-third or 40 percent of the congregation disappear, it is unconscionable…. You can't do nothing. Whatever it is that you try, at least you will be able to stand before Christ one day and say we gave it our best shot…. We never quite figured it out, but we certainly did try!

Through all the good, the bad, and the ugly…through all the unknowns, failures, and successes…through the joys and sorrows, it is worth it! As our culture radically changes, the church must change. For some it may mean launching a new worship gathering and ministry in an existing church. For some it may mean making changes in their existing ministries. For some it may mean birthing a new church.

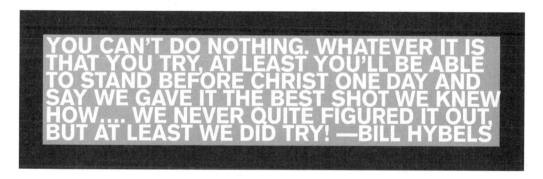
YOU CAN'T DO NOTHING. WHATEVER IT IS THAT YOU TRY, AT LEAST YOU'LL BE ABLE TO STAND BEFORE CHRIST ONE DAY AND SAY WE GAVE IT THE BEST SHOT WE KNEW HOW…. WE NEVER QUITE FIGURED IT OUT, BUT AT LEAST WE DID TRY! —BILL HYBELS

We desperately need both church planters and bridge builders in existing churches, individuals who will help morph modern churches into new territory. I am optimistic that many modern churches can change and that we can see new communities of faith and expressions of worship birthed within them and through them.

That is what this book is all about. We will discuss the pros and the cons. We will hear pioneering stories and see clear examples from churches all around the country that have already been down this road.

Avoiding Superficial Change

This book follows the same format as my earlier book, *The Emerging Church: Vintage Christianity for New Generations*. The first part of this book is a look at the architecture and framework behind the new worship gatherings and ministries. We will discuss reasons why and why not to start this. We will talk through specific steps you can take when starting new worship gatherings in your church. We will walk through critical questions to ask before you start and even if you have already started. We will discuss how to build a team of volunteers who design and create the worship gatherings even with little or no budget.

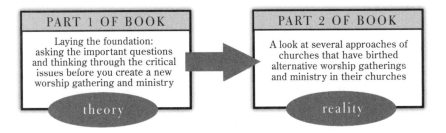

PART 1 OF BOOK	PART 2 OF BOOK
Laying the foundation: asking the important questions and thinking through the critical issues before you create a new worship gathering and ministry	A look at several approaches of churches that have birthed alternative worship gatherings and ministry in their churches
theory	reality

In the second half of this book, we will walk through different approaches churches have taken in birthing new forms of ministry for emerging generations. We will learn from them and note the different options. We'll see how their leadership structure is designed and what the roles of pastors and senior pastors are. We'll get a glimpse of what their worship gatherings and ministries look like throughout the week.

We will hear about the mistakes and lessons learned from leaders in these emerging churches as they explored new worship expressions and made changes. There is a lot to learn from them!

The feeling that Our Emerging Church May Never Emerge

In our story, I clearly remember the time Josh Fox, Rollyn Zoubek, and I spent almost an entire day praying together as we first thought of creating the "Graceland" worship services and ministry at Santa Cruz Bible Church. Santa Cruz Bible Church is a large modern contemporary evangelical church. It was a wonderful, thriving church. Yet, all of us in youth ministry knew something was changing among emerging generations.

It got to the point where we felt that God asked us to rethink church a bit and experiment with some new expressions and forms of worship. We sat on my living room floor, opened the Scriptures, and on index cards wrote down passages that described what a new type of worship service and ministry might look like.

As we started dreaming and writing things down, it became very clear that what we were envisioning was radically different from what our church normally did. Change how you preach? Preaching was the centerpiece of our church! How could we possibly look at a worship gathering more as a holistic experience without preaching as the centerpiece?

Bring in prayer stations, incense, and candles? In our contemporary church that would feel like a huge step backward. We could have been considered to be going Catholic in an evangelical church!

Pay attention to the room we meet in to design more of a sacred space that reflects the ancient? But our building was brand-new and contemporary. Why would we want to

"By faith Jacob, when he was dying, blessed each of Joseph's sons, and worshiped as he leaned on the top of his staff."
—Hebrews 11:21

hide the brand-new contemporary architecture?

Put the band in the back of the room? But don't all worship bands need to be up front and in the lights?

The senior pastor won't be the preacher in these new worship services? How the heck is that going to be allowed? A more communal form of leadership? But aren't decisions made from the top down and then teams implement the vision, not create it? We were doomed. This new worship gathering would never happen, we thought.

Our Safety Net of Confidence

With each card we wrote things on, it seemed more and more obvious that our emerging church ideas might not get the chance to emerge. They were just too different! It felt like they would stay mere dreams and thoughts written on index cards. But I distinctly remember turning to Acts 5:38-39, which says, "Leave these men alone! Let them go! For if their purpose or activity is of human origin, it will fail. But if it is from God, you will not be able to stop these men; you will only find yourself fighting against God."

I actually wrote that passage on a index card. As I did, the sinking feeling — that the emerging service and ministry were doomed before they were even presented — lifted. I was reminded that this was not Dan's or Josh's or Rollyn's thing. This was God's thing! If God was in this, and if he wanted a new emerging form of ministry to be birthed in our church, then it was up to him to make it happen. We would have to do our part, of course. If our ideas were of human origin then they would fail. But if they were of God, no matter how crazy they may sound, then they would happen.

In our particular story, it did happen. Not without struggle, but it happened. We started Graceland as a Sunday night worship gathering for "young adults." Eventually, it morphed into an all-age worship gathering. After several years we ended Graceland. Once again, we morphed into a brand-new church — Vintage Faith Church (we'll talk more about this in Chapter 13).

It's Not Our Emerging Church, But Jesus' Emerging Church!

In the emerging church, we must remember we are not doing the emerging. It is the church of Jesus Christ we are talking about. He is the head of the church (Ephesians 1:21-22), and that means he is head of the emerging church! We must approach all of this very carefully. We cannot have cocky attitudes—thinking we are trying to prove something. We must not do this for the sake of trying to be hip and do something different than whatever else is currently happening in our church. Instead, we are rethinking what form Jesus' church in our emerging culture will be like. That is no light task. We must take it seriously.

This task of designing the emerging church, new worship gatherings, and different ministries must be one that drives us to our knees. It is one that we cry out to God for, asking him to reveal if he is in this, or if it is simply our own "human origins" and personal desires. And as we do that, the burden is lifted. We are simply servants of the King. He will decide if he wants us to start something new or not.

I personally take great refuge in that. As we experiment with creating worship gatherings, we need to always remember it isn't about us and our dreams — it is about Jesus and his Church. It isn't about being creative — it is about Jesus and his Church. It isn't about rethinking our churches — it is about Jesus and his Church. With that in mind, our hearts and attitudes should reflect this truth whether things get rough or things go well!

There is security in knowing that if what we do is of God, then it will happen. Now let's look at some reasons why we should or shouldn't be starting alternative worship gatherings and new forms of ministry in our churches.

Emerging Thoughts

1. Are you comfortable with the fact that emerging worship gatherings are not neat, figured out, and packaged, but rough, pioneering new ground for most churches?

"Oh, brother or sister, God calls us to worship, but in many instances we are in entertainment, just running a poor second to theaters."
—A. W. Tozer

Are you ready to experience possible struggle and misunderstanding in launching something like this?

2. What other options might you pursue if you didn't start an emerging worship gathering? What will you say when you meet Jesus face to face and need to give an account for why you didn't at least try?

CHAPTER 3

Why this is a dangerous book to read

A prudent man sees danger and takes refuge, but the simple keep going and suffer for it.
—Proverbs 22:3

I use the word "dangerous" in the chapter title not to be dramatic or sensationalistic. Nor do I use the word in a positive way, as some have, to suggest we pray "dangerous prayers." I use the word to sound a serious warning as this book begins.

The title of this book is *Emerging Worship: Creating Worship Gatherings for New Generations.* That is exactly what we are will be talking about. But if we jump into creating worship gatherings without thinking about how they fit within the church holistically, we are heading for danger. Let me explain.

I am in regular conversation with pastors and church leaders around the country who notice the growing trend of emerging generations missing from their churches. They probably hear the subtle (or not so subtle) grumblings from young people in their churches about the worship services not connecting with them. Emerging generations in our churches today desire a different kind and form of worship experience to express their worship to God. These are very real issues that we in leadership face today in our emerging culture. We cannot just brush them off or ignore them. We grow concerned about this problem and want to do something about it. This book addresses ways the emerging church is answering these cries. It speaks to the disturbing trends we see as emerging generations disappear from churches at an alarming rate.

This book focuses on the weekend worship gatherings that many churches are starting.

But this book is dangerous if it encourages you to believe that the worship gathering is the most important thing you do each week.

We in church leadership have a natural response when we realize certain demographics (whether age or mindset) are missing in our church. We have been conditioned and trained to immediately think of tweaking our weekend worship service or starting a new gathering.

Over and over again, I hear people asking "How do we start a new postmodern worship gathering?" or saying "We are starting a new emerging church gathering."

This is the absolutely wrong place to begin thinking about all of this. It's not our fault, however, when we think this way — since the primary way leaders view churches today is through the lens of the weekend worship service. It is ingrained in our thinking that the weekend worship service is the primary vehicle and focus for what "church" is. Therefore, as we think of doing something to engage the emerging culture and generations, we immediately think of the worship service.

Most people in our churches likewise view the weekend worship service as their primary focal point. It is their experience of what "church" is. It's not their fault for thinking this way either. We taught them! I once was in a worship service in which the pastor repeated throughout his sermon that the weekend worship service was the most important meeting of everyone's week. So, it's only natural for us in leadership, and for those in our churches, to have our thoughts jump immediately to what we can do in a worship gathering designed for emerging generations. This book is about such worship gatherings. But that is where it can be dangerous.

My fingers are nervously twitching as I write because I am worried that a book that focuses on the weekend worship gathering communicates that church = weekend worship gathering. That is far from the scriptural reality of what church is. Church is the people of God on a mission (1 Corinthians 12:27, Acts 1:8)—people who spend most of their time outside of the weekend worship gathering. So, I need to state up front that the weekend worship gathering is but one part of a holistic church experience.

The average person is awake 112 hours a week (assuming he or she sleeps eight hours a night). If a person goes to a weekend worship gathering that lasts two hours, then 98.2 percent of their week is not in a weekend worship gathering. To most people, "church" involves only 1.8 percent of their time. The rest is supposedly not "church." This is pretty crazy because in reality you and I and other Christians are the Church 100 percent of the time.

We cannot focus primarily on what to do stylistically, methodologically, or philosophically in the weekend worship gathering. We first need to ask what the "church" is. Then we need to ask how the weekend worship gathering fits within the church's life and spiritual formation.

From the old nursery rhyme we were taught to use our hands to form a building while saying, "This is the church, this is the steeple, open the doors, and see all the people." This is wrong! Even our childhood rhymes ingrained in us the idea the church is merely a building we go to once a week rather than who we *are* everyday.

The weekend worship gathering is not the most important thing in someone's week. It's not even the most important thing we in leadership do each week. If we think it is, then we are missing what the Church really is. Then we have been teaching people the wrong definition and giving them a false experience of what "church" is. We need to recognize that most of the process of spiritual formation and mission happens in the 98.2 percent of everyone's week. We better really think about the rest of people's weeks, not just the 1.8 percent they spend in a weekend worship gathering.

What do we mean when we use the word "church"? Our definition will set

"Therefore, since we are receiving a kingdom that cannot be shaken, let us be thankful, and so worship God acceptably with reverence and awe, for our 'God is a consuming fire.'"
—Hebrews 12:28-29

some parameters for the weekend worship gatherings that are the focus of this book.

The Church Isn't:	The Church Is:
A "place" or a building you go to	Disciples of Jesus wherever they are
The weekend meeting where a sermon is delivered and some songs are sung	Groups of disciples meeting in homes and other smaller settings throughout the week who may also gather in a larger meeting to worship together on Sunday
Christians who go to a weekend meeting to get their religious goods and services	The worshipers of a local body on a mission together
Christians who go to "church" on weekends to get their inspiration and feeding for the week	The people of God who are passionately dependent upon God in worship and prayer all week long
Christians who ask, "What does this church have to offer me?"	Disciples of Jesus who ask, "How can I contribute and serve this local body in its mission?"
A place where Christians go to have the pastors do "spiritual" things for them	A community where the pastors and leaders equip the people for the mission and to serve one another
A place to bring your children and teenagers for their spiritual lessons while you receive your sermon and sing a few songs	A community where leaders help train you to teach your children the ways of God and incorporate children and youth into the community so they aren't isolated

Do you see the difference?

Again, this book could be dangerous if you end up believing that the worship gathering of a "church" is the most important thing every week. It is important! But let's start rethinking what we have turned "church" into, both in our minds and in the minds of those in our churches. It is dangerous to elevate the gatherings over true spiritual formation. We need to first have a holistic view of spiritual formation and of the purpose of the church.

Then we will be able to see how our weekend worship gathering fits within that. Only then will we know the importance it does or does not have in bearing fruit.

This book is dangerous if it causes you to spend 80 percent of your time on what produces only 20 percent of one's spiritual growth

If you attend enough church growth conferences, you eventually hear about the Pareto Principle. It is taught in regards to church growth and basic time management principles. Basically, the Pareto Principle is a general rule that says 80 percent of results flow from only 20 percent of our efforts.

Considering this, we in church leadership typically agree that 80 percent of true discipleship and spiritual growth occurs from mentoring, smaller group gatherings, relationships, serving, etc. I also bet (if we are brutally honest) that probably only 20 percent of discipleship really is a result of our weekend gatherings. So it is rather ironic that in most churches we pour 80 percent of our energy and resources into something that produces only 20 percent of long-term spiritual growth.

I recently got into a heated discussion with someone who disagreed with me on this point. This person said that worship services are the most important thing in a Christian's life. This is because the sermon is critical to "feed the flock" and "pastor" the people. I agree that the sermon can be an important part of one's spiritual formation. But let's not overstate its importance! Sermons do provide short-term motivation for people and can inspire individuals to desire further spiritual growth. Sermons can move people in a particular direction and help individuals decide to pursue something. However, it is rare to talk to someone who says his or her life was changed due to a sermon. People may say "Great sermon!" or "I enjoyed that!" right after a weekend service and we can feel self-assured we have accomplished something. But what about a week later? What about two weeks later? They were moved by a sermon, learned insights, and were even inspired — but most people cannot even remember the sermon they heard three weeks ago. (It is even more interesting that many pastors cannot remember what they preached three weeks ago!)

What people do say is that their life was changed by a person who loved them, who helped them through a problem, who talked with them about the Christian life and helped them understand how the Spirit of God changes people. They do remember meeting in a home where they focused on the Scriptures and participated in discussion about the Bible in community. They do remember times of quiet with God where they "fed themselves" in the Scriptures. They do remember specific times when the Spirit moved in their life as they read and meditated upon the Scriptures.

I challenge you to ask people in your church what the sermon was about two weeks ago. Not just the topic, but the Scriptures, principles, and application points. You might be surprised by what you hear! My hope is that you will rethink how much weight you give your sermon and weekend worship gathering.

Please, please do not think I am downplaying the teaching of the Bible! I still preach weekly in weekend worship gatherings. I am very much a Bible-enthusiast and Bible lover. I know the Scriptures are alive and active (Hebrews 4:12) and the Scriptures are inspired by God. I know it is critically important for people to know the Scriptures, and to saturate our hearts and minds in the Scriptures. That is why I am so passionate about making sure the Bible is being taught and learned in the *most effective* ways possible for true spiritual formation to occur. And that is precisely why I think we need to re-look at the long-term impact that our weekend worship gatherings have. I think we need to revisit and rethink where we are spending most of our efforts and hours and hours of time each week. I believe in the emerging church, if we are serious about spiritual formation and serious about Bible teaching, then we need to rethink if what we are doing is the most effective way of teaching for actual life-change. Where do we hear lives are changed the most? That is where we need to put 80 percent of our focus.

If Jesus were to look at how we spend our time during the week and how much we think, worry, and make plans regarding the weekly worship service, what would he say to us? How much time would Jesus spend sitting in an office designing a worship gathering? How much time would he spend on other aspects of spiritual formation and the mission of making disciples? These are the questions I think we need to ask in the emerging church if we are serious about making disciples.

This book is dangerous if it causes you to build your church's foundation upon the weekend worship gathering

I know that we do not build ministry and church on anything but Jesus. Jesus Christ is the head of the church (Colossians 1:18) as I mentioned in the last chapter. *"And God placed all things under his [Jesus Christ's] feet and appointed him to be head over everything for the church, which is his body, the fullness of him who fills everything in every way."* — Ephesians 1:22-23

Jesus gave us a mission to be his church and that is what we should build on — the mission, not the worship service. I am fairly convinced that most churches build on the worship service, however, despite the fact that they have a mission statement. Let me explain graphically what I mean.

Building a church upon the foundation of the weekend worship service

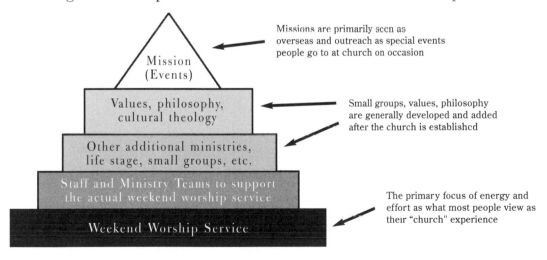

This teaches "church" = the weekend worship service. This is why we hear people say, "I go to church."

Most churches start by building a team to launch a weekend worship service, whether their goal is to plant a new church or begin a new worship gathering for emerging generations. Yes, we build teams and have small groups, but in reality what drives us, and what drives the church, is building on the large weekend service. Everything else is secondary to that. We might draft a statement of our ten core values or incorporate the doctrinal statement from our denomination. But really, it's all built upon the foundation of keeping the weekend worship service going.

Generally the weekend worship service is designed around the preaching and teaching of the senior pastor. (If this is a youth ministry, the weekly youth meeting focuses on the teaching of the youth pastor.) The primary leader of the church focuses most of his or her time on the "worship service." From here we then add other secondary ministries ministry to support the main ministry — the weekend worship service. All these supportive ministries are designed to move more people into the main worship services.

Whatever our church's vision or mission statement, the fact is we hire most of our staff to support the weekend event. We spend most of our budget on the weekend event. A successful church is to us a growing weekend event.

I question this whole traditional line of thinking. This ultimately can produce a consumer form of Christianity and teaches people in our churches to focus their Christian experience around the weekend worship service.

Have we taught people to think they haven't experienced "church" this week if they didn't go to the worship service?

I believe we need to look at church more like this.

Building a church upon the foundation of the mission

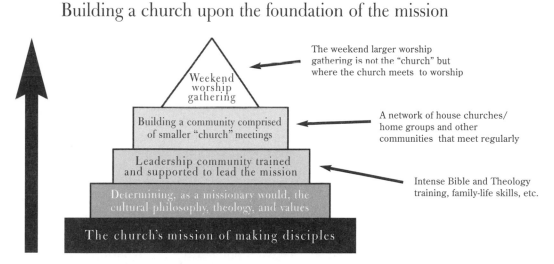

The weekend larger worship gathering is not the "church" but where the church meets to worship

A network of house churches/ home groups and other communities that meet regularly

Intense Bible and Theology training, family-life skills, etc.

Weekend worship gathering

Building a community comprised of smaller "church" meetings

Leadership community trained and supported to lead the mission

Determining, as a missionary would, the cultural philosophy, theology, and values

The church's mission of making disciples

Creates the ethos of a common mission and teaches the people of God on a mission – the church. People say, "We are the church during the week, and we all gather together for worship on the weekend." Individuals ask, "How can I contribute to the mission of this church community?" rather than "What programs and services does this church have to offer me?"

This way of building starts with the mission Jesus gives us (Matthew 28:19, Acts 1:8). It all has to start with defining the mission. The mission is not to start a worship service. The mission is to make disciples.

We then move from this foundation to determine what philosophy, values, and approaches to theology and teaching will apply to the culture in which we serve as missionaries. This is why it is important to study and understand the post-Christian culture in which we are immersed.

We can then develop staff and leadership communities who share the church's mission and help shape its values. Finally, we need to create smaller communities for people to really experience "church." These may be house churches, small groups, meetings in the workplace where Jesus is the focus, etc. Church happens anywhere people are gathered in his name.

We need to recognize this and understand this. It is not dependent on people coming to our building and sitting in our meeting. After we think through the other building blocks, we can begin to design a worship gathering. To do this backwards is dangerous and will ultimately produce consumer-Christians who "go to church" (a worship service), are not engaged in the mission, and don't see themselves as the church.

You may say, "We know our mission isn't to start a worship service." You need to probe and ask if you really do know that. What comes to your mind when you imagine "success"? Is it a view of people all gathered in a worship service you have created? Or is it a view of a community of worshipers being missionaries in their world, being part of community in smaller settings, and then coming together for a worship gathering? There is a huge difference between the two! Probably what comes to your mind and heart first is what you are building on.

This book is dangerous if it ends up putting your focus on the worship service instead of all that happens and is foundational below that.

This book is dangerous if it causes you to slip into the American Idol approach to worship

On one popular TV show, a panel of judges critiqued various singers competing for the title of the next *American Idol.* I wonder if we in church leadership have slipped into trying to become the next American Church (or megachurch) Idol?

We can easily get caught up trying new worship tricks and cool innovative things in our worship gatherings. We can easily desire to have the best technology, the best sound systems, and the best videos. We can try to impress and please those who sit and watch what we do. This *American Idol* approach to "church" reduces us to performers and reduces church attendees to mere judges.

In the emerging church, there is great danger if the focus of our worship gatherings subtly shifts to our video backgrounds, prayer stations, ancient creeds, candles, artwork, etc. If that happens, we'll begin teaching people (without saying it) that the worship service is a service we provide for people. We'll also teach them to come and judge us like the *American Idol* panel does. We might have some nice Paula Abduls who tell us that everything was great even if it wasn't. We might have some

Simons who lash out in criticism about the artwork not being good or not having prayer stations this week. We'll become victims of our own doing if we do not start from and retain a missional emphasis and let everyone know that.

What comments do you hear about your worship service? Do people say, "I enjoyed that" or "That was fun" or "Good job today"? Or do they say, "I encountered God here today" or "I appreciated that people prayed for me here" or "I felt the presence of Jesus here"? There is a big—no,huge—difference between the two.

I recently read comments written by a person who had attended a church worship gathering in a large evangelical contemporary church. It was amazing to read what he wrote about the pastor who was speaking: "1) great delivery; 2) great gestures (not distracting); 3) well organized—the doxology should be done at each service." We have turned our worship gatherings and preaching into a performance! I understand that, in large settings especially, communicating does need certain skill sets developed, but the written comments above mentioned nothing about the heart, the Scriptures themselves, or people's responses. They were merely performance-based observations. We have done a good job training people to view their worship gathering as a spectator event to critique!

We need to guard against creating this kind of consumerism.

I love larger worship gatherings!

You may find it unusual that in a book about creating emerging worship gatherings, I start with some negative things about worship services. I need to simply because they have been a primary reason why there are so many consumer-Christians. Yet, it doesn't have to be like that!

Larger worship gatherings can be beautiful expressions of community worship to God. Personally, I have been part of a church community that has had them for many years. I want to be part of a church where we have true community in smaller settings, but where we also gather in larger meetings.

Those larger meetings are what I primarily describe in this book. I believe the Holy Spirit uses the larger worship gathering as an important part of our spiritual formation.

"Because we are not truly worshipers, we spend a lot of time in the churches just spinning our wheels, burning the gasoline, making noise, but not getting anywhere."
— A. W. Tozer

I love larger worship gatherings. I wouldn't be writing a book on them if I didn't!

True, I am concerned about the things mentioned in this chapter. My prayer is that by mentioning them we will all remember that our mission is not to create a worship service, but to make disciples.

We must remember that the church is not about the worship service, preaching, or music. It also is not about any of the multisensory expressions of worship we create. The church is the people of God on a mission together wherever they are — not just when they are in the meetings we design.

We have a holy responsibility to shape people's view of the Christian experience. If we shape it on a faulty foundation, then woe to us.

May we all heed these dangers.

Emerging Thoughts

1. How would you rate your weekend worship service in terms of the percentage of impact it has on people's spiritual formation? What percentage of time do you put into that service in both your thoughts and actual energy?

2. Compared to the "The Church Isn't / The Church Is" chart, how does your current church line up?

3. Do you agree or disagree that one-way forms of preaching have a limited impact on actual learning and life change?

4. After reviewing the two charts showing different ways to build a church, how would you say your current church was built? Is it built on the foundation of the weekend worship service or on the foundation of the church's mission? What would the people of your church say if asked?

5. Can you relate to the *American Idol* approach to church described in this chapter? How does this approach surface in your church?

CHAPTER 4

Reasons to create a New Worship Gathering

For this reason I kneel
before the Father....
— Ephesians 3:14

"Hey Dan! Everyone's starting these new postmodern worship services. We don't want to be left behind here. How do we start one?"

These words came from an enthusiastic pastor. He called to ask for some input on adding a new worship gathering at his church. In the several minutes I spoke with him, I mostly listened to him explain his reason for calling. It was pretty obvious, however, that he was missing the real reasons to start a new service. I probably disappointed him with my answer. I explained that, based on what he had told me, it probably would be better for him not to start something new.

Around the country, a lot of church leaders sense something needs to change. They notice the absence of emerging generations in their churches. These pastors sense in their guts that change is happening. Because they are engaged in the culture and with people, they recognize the limitations of what is traditionally done in our churches. It is not resonating with emerging generations.

These pastors are wrestling with theology, especially ecclesiology, and they wonder how we got to where we are today. How much has been shaped by the Reformation? How much is a product of modernity? How much is really biblical? These are the leaders who should be creating new worship gatherings and pioneering new forms of ministry.

Other pastors hear about other churches starting alternative worship gatherings. They may want to make sure younger people are still happy in their church. They may even be afraid of losing their younger people to a new alternative worship gathering at another church. So they want to start a new "program" to keep up with other churches.

The latter is basically what the pastor I mentioned earlier was asking me about. Starting a new service to "keep up" with others is destined to be a surface ministry only. It's missing the heart of why we should create worship gatherings.

What are the reasons we should create new worship gatherings? What are some reasons we should direct our prayers to the Father, asking him to act through our hopes and dreams?

Here are five compelling reasons why we should start new worship gatherings.

1. You desire to see emerging generations worship God

A primary motivation to start a new worship gathering is our desire to see emerging generations worshiping God. This should be our passion, not to see new people in our churches or to become a hip church. From this desire to see emerging generations worship God a few things will then happen.

As you rethink worship past the surface, you will find that the changes needed for the emerging church and worship go far beyond changing musical styles. It's also not about adding candles. It is about rethinking how we approach our theology of church. This causes a rethinking of our philosophy. That starts a rethinking of how we view our own local church and our roles as leaders. In turn, this causes a rethinking of our values. Rethinking our values causes a rethinking of our strategies which causes a rethinking of our methodologies. This causes a rethinking of spiritual formation, which begins a rethinking of worship. Rethinking worship results in a rethinking of whether or not to start a new worship gathering (or alter an existing one). Finally, we rethink what we actually do in those services.

What is important is that the underlying motive needs to be in your heart and in your mind. You must feel that something is not quite right and that something needs to be changed in our approach in order to participate in holistic worship.

This is true even if you are one of the people in church leadership who does not actually lead or participate in the new worship gathering. You still need to see the "rethinking" going on behind all of this. You can't be afraid of that.

2. You are starting a new worship gathering to be missional

You may be noticing that things are getting a little scary in post-Christian America. You can see a dramatically decreasing percentage of people in emerging generations participating in your church community. This absence of individuals from the emerging generations who know and love Jesus deeply disturbs your soul.

You might be haunted by the words of Jesus, "Go and make disciples of all nations" (Matthew 28:19) or "The harvest is plentiful, but the workers are few" (Matthew 9:37) or his last words before he ascended to heaven, "You will receive power when the Holy Spirit comes upon you; and you will be my witnesses in Jerusalem, and in all Judea and Samaria and to the ends of the earth" (Acts 1:8).

When you read these Scriptures your heart aches for those who don't know Jesus yet. Your heart pumps fast at the thought of leading a church community that desires to be missional and to do something about it together. When I say "missional" I am not simply talking about propositionally speaking about how to get to heaven. Being missional means living out the gospel in all we do, serving others, and embodying the gospel as a church. (For more information, see the chapter on evangelism in my previous book, *The Emerging Church: Vintage Christianity for New Generations*.)

I just spoke with a friend who teaches at a local public high school. He asked his class about Easter and what they would be doing to celebrate it. They all began sharing about family gatherings and trips to see their grandparents. Noticing not one student said they were going to church, he asked them if they knew what Easter was about. They all shared various Easter egg stories. They talked about spring time and the Easter bunny. Not one single person in his class of 25 high school students mentioned Jesus or his resurrection. Not one! He then asked if they knew how Jesus was involved in Easter, and not one student knew, either!

You may scoff at this story. You may think it isn't that way in your area, but don't underestimate what is happening all around us. Usually when I talk about this issue at conferences, several youth pastors or other pastors or leaders will tell me they don't see this in their community. I then ask them a few questions that almost no one has ever considered:

• Can you sincerely say that you ask in-depth questions of and interact with individuals who are part of the non-church-attending emerging generations in your area? Most of the time, when I press leaders, they admit they only understand the mindset of the Christian young people already in their churches. They aren't talking with or building significant relationships with non-Christians. Their conversations are primarily with Christians. That shapes their impression of what is happening in their communities, which actually is a false impression.

• Have you ever done a county-wide or city-wide survey to see what percentage of emerging generations are actually part of the local churches in your area?

Again, most haven't. So I ask them to please (1) contact every local junior high school, high school, and college or university within ten miles of their church to find out exactly how many students live in their area.

Then, I ask them to (2) call every church to find out (a) how many people and (b) how many youth and young adults attend each one.

I also ask them to (3) look at the most recent U.S. census report to find out what percentage of the population in their county or state is 35 years old or younger.

I next ask them to (4) take a realistic look at the percentage of youth and young adults actually attending their church. This should be compared to the overall statistics of how many are in their county. Then, they can tally all the churches in their local area to see the total percentage of all churches combined.

You may resist this, saying we shouldn't be concerned about numbers. I'm not saying this to focus on numbers, per se. If you knew me, you would know that is the last thing I think about in terms of success. I am not trying to make people depressed about the size of their church or youth ministry. Great and wonderful things happen in small churches, often of more quality than what happens in large churches! Numbers, for numbers' sake, are not what I am trying to stress here.

What I am saying is that actually counting the population in your area and in your local churches will vividly sound an alarm. This type of research should not bother us! After all, this is what is taught in seminary when people prepare for the mission field. It's called "culture mapping." In the same way, we need to look more closely at the reality of what is happening in our own communities. Don't be afraid to do what cross-cultural missionaries are taught to do. Look at some raw data!

When we look at this data, many of us will soberly recognize the need to be missional once again. It should a major reason why we're willing to birth new forms of creative worship gatherings. We are on a mission to see new worshipers of God!

The following are very broad terms I hope will be helpful to you:

PRE-CHRISTIAN

Someone who was raised with a basic understanding of "God" and a Judeo-Christian worldview. They may have had some church experience growing up that was primarily boring or dead ritual. So when a church provides a contemporary and relevant church worship service, they return to the church and trust Jesus Christ (or recommit to him). Most megachurches and growing churches today are reaching this group of people.

POST-CHRISTIAN

Someone who was born and raised outside of any church influence and is now heavily influenced by our pluralistic postmodern culture and values. Generally few of their values, morals, or convictions are based on a Judeo-Christian worldview. "Church" either means nothing to them or they dislike it. Spirituality is subjective and individualistic, often an eclectic potpourri of the world's religious beliefs. They usually oppose the idea of joining any organized established religion. They often have strong anti-evangelical sentiments and a lot of stereotypes against Christians in general. Yet they are usually very spiritually-minded people.

DISILLUSIONED CHRISTIAN

Someone who grew up in a modern evangelical church, who left the church dissatisfied with the current way most churches function (with their emphasis on the big weekend worship service being the "church"). A rising percentage of younger people are not drawn to the megachurch philosophy or to the church structures and values that they grew up in (even in smaller churches). They desire to experience a different kind of church and different kind of Christianity than they grew up with.

3. You understand that new models are needed to address both cultural and generational change

I specifically did not say that a new "model" (singular) is needed. I hesitate to even use the word "model" anymore. It immediately indicates that something can be packaged, boxed as a specific set of systems and programs, transported, and then replicated somewhere else. That is not the case with emerging churches. In fact, it is the opposite of what's happening.

When we say a "church model," we are speaking of a "community model." We cannot export and replicate a community of people. Each one is distinct and different. We only dishonor the people in a local church and risk creating a backlash when we blindly use someone else's "model."

There is no one emerging church model. I like to use the term "approaches" to ministry rather than "models." In the future, there will be hundreds of hybrids of various approaches. Why? Because each local church is different.

Furthermore, no matter what approaches work today, the fact is that new approaches will be needed as our culture's worldview continues to change and as brand-new generations emerge.

The following are two dynamics of change we should distinguish as we consider designing worship gatherings:

Worldview change

We are rapidly moving from a modern to a postmodern world and from a Judeo-Christian nation to a post-Christian nation. As a result, we need to develop new approaches to "church." This involves a shift in our worldview, ecclesiology, and epistemology.

Emerging generations are growing up in a completely postmodern world. This drastically affects how they think—it's not just a change in style or preferences. It incredibly affects people's spiritual viewpoints, their understanding of "God," and their thoughts about "Christianity." It affects how people process what they learn and how they think. It affects what forms of communication they use, how they make decisions, and how they relate to one another.

This affects the way we design worship services, and why aesthetics and the creation of a "sacred space" are now important. Preaching must change, evangelism must change, and spiritual formation itself must change. Even leadership needs to change because of this cultural shift.

Generational change

Marked generational change or generation gaps have occurred in cycles throughout American history. This generational change is what most of us thought was going on when we began noticing things were no longer working in our churches. We assumed it was a normal generational change (of music styles, for instance).

To solve this, we tried adapting our music and thought that would solve our problems. "Gen X" churches and ministries began to claim they were "the flock that likes to rock!" This was an attempt to prove to the younger generations that church can be hip, contemporary, and play newer music. We still used the same underlying ministry philosophy, however, that we had with previous generations.

Now that we have Gen Y and Gen Z, we're still assuming that if we simply add some hip-hop music we will be okay. Because it's a matter of generational style change we need to address. This is partially true. But we are also experiencing a massive cultural worldview change that has far broader implications than just musical style.

In the past, when younger people left the church, we knew they would come back when they had kids because their "roots" were there. But today those growing up outside of the church don't have any Christian roots to return to. Merely dealing with generational style issues is not going to work this time around. There is a big difference between worldview change and generational change, and we now face both combined!

4. You want to a be good steward of finances and buildings for the Kingdom

Another important reason for creating a new worship gathering and related ministries in an existing church is to make good usage of the finances the saints in that church have sacrificially given through the years. So often a church building's sanctuary and other rooms are unused most of the week.

5. You see how emerging worship allows intergenerational relationships to develop and keep a church from dying out

Biblically, it is important to cultivate intergenerational relationships among believers (Psalm 145:4).

In new church plants, most people are younger. They miss the beauty of seeing the older mentor the younger. If we're creative, however, all the age groups in a given church can experience community when birthing new worship gatherings and ministries. This is true even when new emerging churches partner with older churches.

If your church is older—and one day may literally die out and close its doors if you don't do something—it's beautiful to allow a godly leader to come in and birth something new.

If your church is very contemporary, attractive to Baby Boomers, and thriving, but fails to see emerging generations become part of your community, fast forward to the future. You too will age and someday die out — if you aren't proactively thinking ahead. I have heard that Europeans probably never imagined their cathedrals would eventually become tourist attractions and sit empty on Sunday — but they have! Don't think the same thing can't happen here.

"For This Reason"

This chapter gives you an idea of the heart behind creating a new worship gathering and related ministries. It shows why it is so important to prayerfully consider doing something in your church.

When we focus our prayers, we should be able to tell the Lord, "For this reason (or for these reasons), we are starting a new worship gathering...." It's essential to clarify what those reasons are! The reasons extend far beyond the five I've discussed above.

Emerging Thoughts

1. If you were to write out a list of the reasons to start a new worship gathering, what would you include in your list?

2. Are there any reasons described in this chapter that you strongly agree or disagree with? Why?

CHAPTER 5

Critical Questions to Ask Before Starting a New Worship Gathering

*Never mistake motion
for action.*
—Ernest Hemingway

I once went hiking in the Grand Canyon for six days. My group booked our camp sites several weeks in advance. Before we left, we read several books and studied trail maps. No one in the group had done this before, so we had a lot of questions to ask and answer in preparation for our expedition. We had to carefully estimate how much water, food, and other supplies to bring for the six days we planned to be in the canyon.

After a lot of preparation, we went to the edge of the canyon, took a good look, and then began slowly hiking down into it with our heavy backpacks. Our trail was narrow and full of switchbacks, so I was glad we had good hiking boots on. The climate was very hot, so I was glad we had brought lots of water, which we knew we had to ration for the duration of the journey.

As we went further down into the canyon, I noticed a small group of middle-aged foreign tourists were out hiking, too. They were joking with one another and took an endless series of pictures along the trail. I immediately noticed they had no backpacks, no hiking boots, no water—just their cameras.

I figured they were going down part way down the trail to get a good feel of the canyon. After all, they seemed confident they knew what they were doing, although I couldn't understand what they were saying since they weren't speaking English.

On any hike, you spread out from other groups and sometimes see them later on. After about four hours, I saw this group again. This time they looked very concerned. They weren't laughing anymore. In fact, two of them seemed to be arguing about what to do. They looked totally wiped out and had no water. Their mouths were dry and the heat of the sun had baked them pretty intensely. In fact, one woman was lying on her back from heat exhaustion.

As we approached them, one man ran over to ask us for water. We gave him some, of course. Through broken English, we learned they thought the trail was taking them to a restaurant. I knew there was a restaurant in the canyon, but it was in another section far away!

It was a sad and rather distressing scene. Park rangers had to be called in. They had to send a helicopter to get this group since night was coming and they definitely didn't have the strength to climb back out of the canyon.

Preparing for the Journey

In many ways, churches who venture to start new alternative worship gatherings sometimes resemble a group of foreign tourists. They're all excited about the idea of reaching emerging generations. They start their journey wide-eyed and full of smiles. They may even take a lot of pictures. But soon things don't go as well as they planned. Or maybe things go better than planned! Then confusion sets in. What do we do now? Who makes the decisions about what to do next?

Usually after a new worship gathering starts and a full-blown ministry develops within an existing church, tensions rise. Individuals haggle over power and control. Feelings get hurt. The worship gathering gets yanked around. And the scores or hundreds of individuals whom God brought together to be part of the new worship gathering ultimately suffer.

I don't mean to sound gloomy if you are starting something new in your existing church. Then again, I have seen too many sad situations happen where church leaders weren't thinking ahead. What could be a wonderful and joyful experience can easily turn confusing and ugly if you don't think through some key issues from the beginning.

In any new movement, transition, or pioneering effort, things don't come easy. If there were a chapter I wish I could have read before we started the Graceland worship gatherings and ministry at Santa Cruz Bible Church, this would definitely be the one! If I had read this chapter, I would have saved myself and other staff members so much personal frustration and grief, so many long and drawn out discussions, so much heartache and misunderstanding and tension.

We are going to walk through the questions everyone needs to ask — and answer — before you start something new in your existing church. Whether you are planting a church or morphing an existing worship gathering, these questions still pertain to you!

Here are 10 critical questions to ask before you start:

1. What is the holistic plan for this new worship gathering as it relates to the whole church?

By far, this is the most important question to answer — the one I hear the most nightmare stories about when it isn't answered properly.

If you are starting something new, it is critical that you clearly define what kind of worship gathering you want to create and who it is for, and then define what your strategy is for fitting this new ministry within the whole church.

In the second part of this book, we examine several different approaches churches

"They worship me in vain; their teachings are but rules taught by men."
—Matthew 15:9

have used to birth new worship gatherings or plant new churches. You will get specific ideas for the various structures and ways churches are doing this.

The person who leads a new worship gathering may envision it as an all-age worship gathering. But the senior pastor (or another staff member) may see people in their thirties or forties attending and become concerned:

- Wasn't the worship gathering supposed to be for people in their twenties?
- Why are people of all ages going?
- Shouldn't they attend the "main" worship services when they turn 30?
- What are they still doing in there?
- Wasn't this supposed to be an "outreach" service designed to get younger people into the church?
- Wasn't our goal to see everyone eventually move into the main worship service?

If these issues aren't thoroughly discussed and agreed upon ahead of time, your dreams can easily turn into nightmares for everyone concerned.

2. What happens in terms of spiritual formation and evangelism beyond the worship gathering?

If your church is truly rethinking church for a post-Christian culture, then you need to rethink all you do—not just the worship service. You need a clear plan for how spiritual formation will take place throughout the week.

What else are people involved in during the week?

How is true community developed outside the worship gathering?

How does evangelism occur?

When we started the Graceland Sunday night worship gatherings at Santa Cruz Bible Church, we gathered 50 people to serve as leaders. They were equipped to serve in various ways according to the way God had designed them.

These 50 individuals also joined new home groups or what might be called home churches. They embraced the fact that these midweek home gatherings were more important for spiritual formation than the larger weekend gathering. In these home groups they ate meals together, opened the Scriptures together, and walked through books of the Bible together. These home groups prayed and shared life together. Older leaders mentored the younger. These groups did service projects together helping the homeless. They took Christmas gifts to needy families in our area. They befriended unbelievers and invited them to join our community of worshipers. These home groups served as the church every day of the week.

The worship gathering on Sunday nights was important, of course! We kept clearly communicating, however, that the home gatherings were really the backbone of all we did. This was ingrained from the beginning, not something we added later.

3. What is the role of the senior pastor and elders or board?

From the beginning, you must think this through very carefully.

There are all types of senior pastors. Some support emerging worship gatherings wholeheartedly without reservation. They trust younger leaders and give them the authority to create something new. Other senior pastors struggle with fear or with power and control issues. In almost every case in which trouble develops in new worship gatherings, it is because the senior pastor decides he wants or "needs" more involvement and control of the gathering.

At first, this might not be an issue. If the new worship gathering grows significantly in number and becomes a central part of the church, however, tensions are likely to arise — if the question of the role of the senior pastor and elders or board is not defined ahead of time.

ADDITIONAL CHAPTERS ONLINE
FOR SENIOR PASTORS

Visit www.vintagefaith.com to read a very important chapter:
"A Personal Plea to Senior Pastors." This additional chapter deals with
this subject of the role of senior pastor in more depth.

At Santa Cruz Bible Church, the senior pastor at the time, Chip Ingram, came to Graceland about once a year or year and a half. He had enough intuition to sense what was going on at Graceland through my relationship with him. Besides, he was plenty busy preaching in the other services. So for the most part, he rarely came to Graceland. He trusted us and didn't feel he was called to or designed for this approach to emerging worship and ministry.

But not all senior pastors are like Chip in giving the freedom he gave us when we first started Graceland. When freedom and empowerment aren't given, then it is only a matter of time before tension and struggle over values occurs. When clear questions aren't thought through and answered in advance, there is a high likelihood of trouble later. Some senior pastors decide to preach at the new worship gathering once a month or every few months. This becomes a rather odd thing in almost every case. Why? Often, they don't take into consideration that these new worship gatherings are designed to speak and relate to different kinds of individuals than those who go to the other ("main") worship services. If they weren't different, after all, you wouldn't need to start a new worship gathering!

We need to remember to rethink preaching for emerging generations and clearly define what the preaching arrangement will be from the start.

The same is true for your church's elders, board, or other leadership structure. This was overlooked with Graceland. We functioned as a college ministry for a year. Then we became a full-fledged, all-age worship gathering and ministry. About three years into it, I had an elder ask me, "Dan, how is the college group going?" Yikes! I realized the elders were not up to speed with what was going on!

It took a lot of communicating to catch them up with what we were doing. It wasn't the elders' fault. They were just so busy with everything else they were doing that they didn't go to Graceland. And I didn't tell them what was happening.

One church I know wisely assigned three elders to be part of their church's new worship gathering and community. These three elders made a commitment to be at all the new worship gatherings and leadership events. They were part of the home groups and other meetings that developed. I wish we had done that at Graceland. That way, the elders would have known the people, been part of the community, and shared its values.

Another church I know selected individuals from the new worship gathering community to be trained by the elders and join them on the board.

In another church, the senior pastor felt it was important for the pastor of the new worship gathering to join their church's board of elders. That way, he could be at all of the elder meetings to represent his ministry. I highly recommend doing the same at your church.

In terms of reporting structure, whether your church has 100 people or 5,000, I think the pastor of the new worship gathering needs to report directly to the senior pastor or directly to the elders or the board. This is different from a life-stage high school pastor, for instance, who may report to the executive pastor. The new pastor and the senior pastor also really need to spend time together often in order to develop a close relationship.

Whatever approach your church decides to take, you need to think through how the highest levels of leadership at your church will relate to your new worship gathering and community.

4. What will be the specific points of integration between the new worship gathering and the rest of the church?

You need to make a written list of the value and philosophy differences between the existing church congregation and the new worship gathering and community. Remember, if cultural change wasn't happening, you wouldn't be starting a new worship gathering. So you want to do everything you can to avoid a detrimental clash of values when the two groups do things together. Let me give you an example.

At Santa Cruz Bible Church, we used to have a five-hour "101: How to Belong" membership class. These classes seemed to be great for most people who attended our church. But when we birthed Graceland, we struggled with this class.

First, to have a class at 9:00 a.m. on a Saturday didn't work with younger adults. If they didn't have kids, they were probably still sleeping. (I know I would be!)

Second, for many growing up in a post-Christian culture, to call something "101" reeks of organized religion. They would wonder why we were using academic and systematized numbers to talk about Jesus. It's not right or wrong, of course; it's just a difference in values!

Beyond that, the environment itself created a clash of values. Talking about becoming part of a spiritual community in a classroom seems contradictory to many in the emerging generations. The "101" method of teaching used PowerPoint slides and fill-in-the-blank notebooks in a lecture format with limited small group discussion. Instead of forcing members of the Graceland community to take this "101" class, we met at my house. We kept the size of the group intentionally smaller, so we could get to know each other better. We shared a meal together. We reworked the teaching materials and changed wording that could come across as either offensive or silly to those we saw as part of our community. We didn't use fill-in-the-blanks. Instead, we gave out materials that discussed our beliefs, presented what it means to become a member, and explained why we even have membership. This was all done in a dialogue format instead of as a presentation. We also walked through the organizational structure of the church to show Graceland was not a separate entity.

This is one example of how you need to carefully examine everything you do when integrating different communities in your church. You need to decide what you can — and can't — do together.

Other important questions to think through:

- Will you have all-church prayer meetings together? If so, how will they be designed to appeal to both groups?
- Will you combine both groups for church picnics, retreats, Christmas services, or any other events?
- Which staff meetings will be all together and which will be held separately?
- What about mission trips?
- What about educational classes?
- How about the budget?
- Will you consider the new worship community a "church plant" that needs to be self-supportive within a certain time period?

5. How will intergenerational relationships be encouraged and developed?

It is critical to develop intergenerational relationships. At Graceland, we bridged the gap by asking older people in our church — mainly in their forties, fifties, sixties, and even seventies — to serve as our home group leaders.

The older people who hosted these home groups had wisdom and life experience. They opened up their homes to take in five to 20 people — primarily people in their twenties and thirties. Some of these home group leaders did not regularly attend the Graceland worship gatherings, but they all had a heart to disciple and shepherd emerging generations.

In addition, many times in the worship gatherings we brought in people in their sixties and seventies to give their testimonies, share how they kept their marriage going for 50 years, or participate in some other way. These times for older individuals to share their wisdom with younger people were always well received.

Always think of how you can bridge generations, whether through mission trips, men's and women's groups, or serving together with the children or another ministry in your church.

6. How will existing children, youth, college, and singles ministries in the existing church be impacted?

One church started a new worship gathering and ministry for emerging generations that, ironically, frustrated the college pastor. The college pastor was using rather modern programs for college ministry. Many college-age people who came to the church's new worship community felt the church's pre-existing college ministry was not in sync with their values and philosophy. This can happen with youth and other ministries, as well.

Rethinking church for emerging generations means rethinking a spectrum of ministries. At Graceland, we didn't think of doing a children's ministry at first. After a while, however, we realized that so many young parents and single moms and dads were bringing their children. So we adjusted the time that we met in order to develop a children's ministry during the worship gathering.

We reformatted the worship gathering so the children could remain in the service for about 20 minutes. That way, they could observe their parents worshiping and experience being part of the community. When it came time for the sermon, we then dismissed them.

As we rethink the church, we also need to rethink how youth ministry is part of it. Interestingly, when I was a high school pastor we had a hard time getting youth to attend the worship service. With Graceland, we had the reverse situation. Graceland drew a lot of teenagers into the worship service. We then had to funnel them into the church's youth ministry.

In the emerging church, youth need to be fully enveloped into full participants in the worship services and life of the church as a whole. Sadly, often the larger a church gets, the more separate the youth and youth ministry become from the life of the church. We end up creating "youth churches" that in many ways stunt their long-term spiritual formation. Many have no church body life experience before they graduate. They're grown up but have no idea what to do in church. Is it any wonder so many opt out of church in their late teens? As we design emerging worship gatherings that are more in tune with our culture today, I'm convinced youth will want to participate.

The more we see families as holistic, the less youth ministry will be isolated. Youth ministries are still important! But they should be missional, help build healthy peer influence and family ministry, and focus on the spiritual formation issues relevant to teens.

7. How will you keep healthy lines of communication between the senior pastor and the rest of the church leadership?

At Santa Cruz Bible Church, we had all-staff meetings every Monday morning. We reviewed the weekend, but the Graceland worship services were never mentioned. The focus was completely on the "main" services of the church. I eventually raised this issue with the senior pastor, who immediately made a change. It was simply oversight — after all, most of the church staff did not go to the alternative worship gathering.

It is important to make sure you communicate on a regular basis with the entire church staff. The same goes for communicating with the elders and board. One time, an elder at Santa Cruz Bible Church was signing receipts and came across a receipt for incense. Incense for a "Bible church" sounded strange. He asked a Graceland staff member for an explanation.

We ended up fielding questions about almost everything we did. Why, for instance, were the stages set up in the back of the room for the worship band (so they would be behind the people and not in the spotlight). Or why we needed to purchase different lighting for our extended stage (so we could be among the people).

This takes a lot of communication and a clear understanding of your vision. We once brought in someone from Leadership Network to speak to our entire staff about postmodernism, which helped them understand why change was needed.

Educating your whole staff on postmodernism and the shift to a post-Christian culture will help you gain their support.

8. What is the strategy and timing for research, team building, and launching?

From the beginning, you need teams in place to help flesh out the emerging church's vision and values. That vision and those values should be determined by the individuals who will be serving in the new worship community.

It could take six months to a year to prepare to launch a new worship gathering and community. In many ways, you have to view this just like a church plant. You need to develop multiple layers of volunteers to serve in their areas of giftedness.

All-church communication is also critical during this time. That way, people who are already part of the other services at your church will know what is happening.

9. If this is a "missional venture," how do you keep it from simply becoming a "happening thing" for those who are already christians in your area?

Right from the beginning, you need to determine whether you view the emerging worship gathering and community as a missional venture. Are you birthing this because you believe in your heart that your church needs to rethink what "church" is? Are you seriously

"If there is no wonder, no experience of mystery, our efforts to worship will be futile." — A. W. Tozer

rethinking how to do things to engage post-Christian culture and emerging generations?

There is a huge difference between that and designing something so younger Christians in your church have a place to go. As I often say, church is not a place you go. Instead, it is a community of worshipers on a mission together. If this principle is not clear in the DNA of what you are doing, it is likely you will create another consumer-oriented gathering. It's that important!

For one, all of the leaders and volunteers need to clearly know the mission and vision of the ministry. Second, you need to know who is coming!

In our setting, from day one, we have had a little communication/prayer card that people filled out when they came to the worship gathering. On the card, we specifically asked, "Are you part of another church? If so, which one?" We also asked if they went to other services in our church. This way we could clearly see how many people were coming that do not belong to any other church. Without this knowledge, we may think great things are happening as numbers swell when, in actuality, we're fueling Christian consumerism.

You can avoid this by making sure you clearly communicate to everyone why you exist and what the vision of the ministry is. Keep track of how many people are in the small groups or home churches that meet midweek. That way you can get an idea of who comes only for the worship gathering. This is a serious thing to watch.

One emerging church met on Sunday nights, but noticed they got a lot of people from other churches. So they canceled their Sunday night time and began gathering on Sunday morning instead. Then they could see who truly belonged to their community.

Another emerging church thought they were doing great in evangelism because so many people were coming to their evening worship gathering. But then they did a survey. It turned out only about 20 percent of the people saw that worship gathering as their church. 80 percent went to some other church and then came to this one as a supplement. If you are missional, this defeats your very purpose.

10. How do you measure success?

In any church, you should have an idea of how you measure success. If you are trying to be evangelistic yet are attracting those who already are Christians, then you better have a way to measure this and make needed changes.

For us, we wanted to know: How many people are being baptized? What percentage of the worship gathering is serving in ministry somewhere? How many leaders are being developed on ministry teams? What percentage of those in the gathering are in midweek home churches or other small groups?

Such measurements need to be monitored and evaluated. Watching these types of statistics will let you know if you are hitting the goals you hope to achieve. You may have a room packed with five hundred people. But does that mean you are being successful? Real success is whether or not our worship gatherings and church as a whole are producing disciples — disciples who are loving God more, and loving people more (Matthew 22:37-39). We need to train ourselves to be evaluating what is most important, not what is only on the surface. We need to train ourselves to be asking the right questions about what we are looking for in terms of results, not just counting people or evaluating our program.

I really hope and pray that if you are starting a new worship gathering, or even have already started one in an existing church, that these questions will cause some evaluation and stir healthy conversation.

Emerging Thoughts

1. Are there any questions you have missed in the development of your emerging worship gathering? If so, which questions?

2. If you leave any of these questions unanswered, how could they lead to trouble in the future? What can you do now to address these concerns?

CHAPTER 6

First Steps toward Starting a New Worship Gathering

*A prudent man gives
thought to his steps.*
—Proverbs 14:15

I recently spoke with a pastor who was a little dismayed. He had started a new worship gathering in his church, but it never took off and they were closing it down.

I began asking some questions. It turned out he had gone to a conference where they talked about starting emerging worship gatherings. He went back home and bought candles and other gothic décor. He started a worship service about two weeks later. A few people came, but the pastor and his wife were absolutely exhausted since they did most of the work. The people who came did not understand the vision and weren't even sure what to expect. Not surprisingly, it soon shut down with a wiped-out and disappointed pastor.

Starting a new worship gathering in your church is not a light matter or an easy task. You need to view it as birthing a new church in terms of the degree of preparation that must take place beforehand.

If you have already started something in your church, please go through this chapter quickly to ensure you are taking each matter seriously.

1. Make prayer and developing a prayer team your two top priorities

As obvious as this seems, it is often neglected with tragic results. Almost every time I talk to someone who has launched a new worship gathering, I ask how they have incorporated prayer in their planning. Usually, the leader prayed and sometimes they had their team pray. But prayer is rarely seen as a foundation.

I once attended a church known for having more than 2,000 younger people in its worship service. When I met their lead prayer person, however, she told me that only three individuals served on their prayer team. "It's tough to get anyone to pray," she told me. I was rather stunned and then saddened that two years later this church went through some very sad situations and was well below half its previous size.

We greatly underestimate the role of prayer in birthing or doing ministry. This is a serious danger. Jesus Christ clearly said, "Apart from me, you can do nothing" (John 15:5). Jesus told his disciples to ask the Lord of the harvest to send workers into the harvest field (Matthew 9:38). The constant thread in the early church was prayer. Yet we have become so accustomed to relying on our own methodology. Because we have the art and science of church growth mastered, we think, we subtly push prayer to the sidelines.

When we started Graceland, a young man named John Biggs came to talk with me. After he heard the vision for this new ministry, he felt it was so crazy that it would work only if God stepped in. So John volunteered to start a prayer ministry. Before Graceland started, we had a core group of people pray together every week for an hour. Of the 50 leaders in place when we started, 20 were on that prayer team. I saw this faithful group of 20 people on their knees praying for Graceland every week for an hour before the worship gathering began. To this day, I dread to think what would have happened if John had not started that prayer group. Sadly John died of cancer at the age of 26, but his legacy of prayer encourages us to this day.

For Vintage Faith Church, we now have taken this even further. Before we had a single meeting about the church, we developed an e-mail list of 150 people who committed to pray for the birth of the new church. These people see Vintage Faith Church as a missional venture, just as missional as anyone going overseas.

Each Monday, I send an e-mail with specific prayer requests as well as reports on how things are going. Someone also stepped in to begin a weekly prayer group for Vintage Faith Church — just like John Biggs did with Graceland.

Can Your Church be Explained Without the Holy Spirit?

You may know intellectually that prayer is important. But now I'm bluntly asking if you not only know it, but practice it? Any new worship gathering needs to be bathed in prayer. May we never think we can do this on our own!

A core value for Vintage Faith Church is that we can't explain what happens with the church by the methodology we use. It can be explained only by the Holy Spirit's involvement.

Someone once questioned how much of the megachurch movement could be sociologically explained without the Holy Spirit. Interesting question! We have gotten so darn smart in our churches (seriously!). We have figured out a lot about how people function. We know how they respond to our felt-need programming, easy and friendly parking lot traffic flow, and easy sign-ups for various programs. We have mastered the exact psychological and demographical marketing plans needed to draw people to what we have to offer them.

We can get people in our church buildings. They may even take steps to change their life by putting into practice the four steps we give in our sermons. Apart from human innovation and a clever understanding of human psychology, however, can we explain why we now see people flock to many megachurches (much the same way they flock to Wal-Mart or Disneyland)?

How do we know that what happens in our churches is not the result of human work and clever thinking alone? How do we sense the Holy Spirit's involvement? Are we drawing our energy for what we do out of Romans 6-8, or do we rely more on our own methodologies, programming, and how-to principles?

What part of your church can be explained only as a result of the working of the Holy Spirit? Remember, large numbers are not necessarily a sign of the Holy Spirit. Marilyn Manson has sold millions of CDs. Every weekend, tens of thousands of people go to movies the Holy Spirit would surely not approve of (and it must grieve him!). I could sponsor and promote a keg party on the beach and probably have several hundred people show up. Numbers alone do not mean the Holy Spirit is involved.

Now I hope there are hundreds of people in your church, perhaps even thousands! I am all for large churches and megachurches! I have been part of a very large church for the past fifteen years. So I am not against them by any means. I just have an unsettling feeling about how "smart" we get and how little the Spirit and prayer are mentioned in our endeavors.

In the emerging church, we must depend on the power of the Holy Spirit. We must be dependent upon God for all we do in our worship gatherings.

I know this is a "I know we are supposed to pray" question I am asking, but the question is — are you?

2. Evaluate your local mission field and context

All missionaries going overseas are taught to study the culture of where they are going. They learn the language, the demographics, and the spiritual beliefs of who they are going to bringing the message of Jesus to. They desire to know the best way to communicate, to engage in conversations and relationships with them.

We have learned through a lot of mistakes in cross-cultural missions that to implement American "church" and ministry as done in America overseas in a foreign culture does not work. It is best to develop a church that engages the culture (not sins nor compromises the message of Jesus, but engages the culture) in a manner which relates to the people.

Develop friendships with non-believers before you begin. I think in starting a new

"When a person, yielding to God and believing the truth of God, is filled with the Spirit of God, even his faintest whisper will be worship."
—A. W. Tozer

ministry and worship gathering in our emerging post-Christian culture, we too often think we are starting something for modern thinking people with a Judeo-Christian worldview. If we do this, we are not thinking like missionaries. I suggest making sure that whoever is leading the ministry is in a friendship with post-Christian non-believers whom they can ask and talk to about their beliefs and their feelings about church. I am constantly amazed, when I probe church leaders, to find that so many do not have relationships with non-believers.

I would also be in a place where you can have focus groups to be able to listen and learn from those you are hoping to see become part of your church community. I would bring a non-Christian into your leadership training and give him or her the time to share with your leaders their perspective and have your leaders even ask questions of them. If you have friendships with non-believers, this is not a problem to do! If you can't think of anyone you could even ask to do this, then maybe you aren't engaged with the minds of those you hope to see come to know Jesus through what you are doing.

Do a demographic survey of who lives in your town or city. I covered this specifically with examples of what to do in chapter 4, "Reasons to Create a New Worship Gathering." I would make sure you have a good feel of who lives in your community, and what is the spiritual climate of your community. Don't assume you know who is there in your community until you actually can say you know what percentage goes to evangelical churches, what percentage might be Buddhist, what are the ages and population makeup of your community, how many high school and college students are there, etc.

3. Select a vision-based team that will serve in their areas of giftedness

In addition to taking a look at your community, you need to take a look at who you are! A big decision you need to make is who will start the new worship gathering and ministry. That team should be composed of individuals who already instinctively sense why such a gathering is needed and desire to be part of the new community.

If a solo pastor thinks of starting something new and designs and plans the gathering by himself, the heart of what emerging generations are seeking in worship and in church will probably be missed.

In the emerging church, the days of the solo leader are gone. We still need leadership. We still need decisions being made. But we need to approach all emerging worship gatherings and ministries with much more of a community approach. It can't be based on the gifts of one or two people. Instead, you'll want to form several teams that will be involved from the beginning. I'll discuss this further in chapter 8.

4. Why former youth pastors are usually ideal for starting a new worship gatherings

I led the high school ministry at Santa Cruz Bible Church for eight years before we started Graceland. As a youth pastor, I was engaged in the thinking and culture of youth. I wasn't removed from what was happening in the emerging culture or in the minds of youth. This attention to youth culture, in fact, is how I noticed a huge cultural shift begin to take place. It was a natural transition for me to begin the Graceland worship gatherings. Eventually, I phased out of direct youth ministry.

Most emerging worship gatherings are going to reflect the values of youth as they grow older. When a former youth pastor becomes the person who spearheads a new worship gathering, she can easily stay connected to the culture she knows.

If you are starting a new worship gathering inside an existing church, you may want to having your youth pastor become your new leader. He or she already has a network of relationships, understands the church, and knows the senior pastor and elders or board.

5. Determine which of your values are different from the rest of the church's

A critical mistake I often hear from church leaders who start a new worship gathering is retaining the existing church's "core values." We want to have a sense of connection. Yet if we insist that the church's values and philosophy remain the same in the new emerging worship gathering, we are not clearly thinking through the changes happening in our culture.

Ask any missionary: the values of one culture do not automatically transfer to another culture. It's just as true here as overseas. America's modern culture is radically different from today's postmodern culture.

For instance, many modern churches make "doing ministry with excellence" a core value. Now, making sure that ministry is done well in the emerging church is not a bad thing. Most emerging churches value the effort to ensure the quality of what is done in worship gatherings. But "excellence" is not a core value in the emerging church. If it lacks authenticity or is too perfect and polished, "excellence" can actually go against the grain of emerging church values.

Another example of value differences shows up in the design of worship gathering spaces. In most contemporary modern churches, a high value is placed on the preacher and worship leader being prominent and easy to see (usually on a platform stage). In many emerging churches, a high value is placed on not being prominent or on a platform.

Different values for different groups of people

Then there's the issue of what belongs next to the worship gathering space. One church wanted to build a new building. A discussion was held about the placement of the church's bookstore and coffeehouse. The emerging church leader wanted to put the coffeehouse as close to the worship gathering space as possible. He valued community and connection as the focus and priority for life change. The decision was made, however, to build the bookstore closest to the worship space. Other church leaders felt that the church's books and recordings are the most important catalysts for life change.

Please think through value differences and recognize there should be value differences! If there weren't, you wouldn't need a new worship gathering and ministry.

Emerging Thoughts

1. If you are starting an emerging worship gathering in an existing church, ask your-

"As worship begins in holy expectancy, it ends in holy obedience. Holy obedience saves worship from becoming an opiate, an escape from the pressing needs of modern life."
—Richard Foster

self, "How is prayer incorporated in the life of my existing church?" Do you want the prayer model of your existing church to be for the same for the new worship gathering and ministry? Why or why not?

2. How will the demographic and cultural realities in your area affect the way you approach your new ministry?

3. What values will be different?

CHAPTER 7

Common Values in Emerging Worship Gatherings

Let everything that has breath praise the LORD.
— Psalm 150:6

"What do one of these emerging worship gatherings look like?"

"What do you do in them that makes them different than what we already do in our church?"

"What exactly happens in them?"

I'm often asked these questions, but there is no answer. The reason there is no answer is there is no model of an emerging worship gathering because each one is unique to its local church context, community, people, and specific leaders of the church. Each worship gathering is a different size, and that also changes how things happen. Each one meets in a different space and that changes things.

So I can't give an answer to what one looks like, as there is no one precise answer. But we can talk about some common values and give some description of how these values are being lived out.

The values listed here are in no particular order but are common to churches across the United States. It is fascinating when you hear some of the same values in emerging worship happening in Florida and Ohio, California and Minnesota. It says that this is not a local change, but something much bigger than that.

These Examples Are to *Stimulate Thinking and Creativity, Not Simply Duplicate*

"When the offerings were finished, the king and everyone present with him knelt down and worshiped."
—2 Chronicles 29:29-30

As we consider emerging worship gathering values in this chapter, please understand this is not something to read and then try to duplicate in your church. Each local church should design a worship gathering that is unique to its church and community. Still, I believe considering examples and ideas from other churches, so we can see what they are doing, is a good thing! We can learn, we can gather ideas, we can get inspired. We can see glimpses of what others do to stimulate our own creativity.

I love being part of various worship gatherings and reading about what other churches are doing. It helps us in our context to consider ideas and then determine which worship forms fit who we are. That is what I hope this chapter and additional ideas in the rest of this book will do for you — stimulate your thinking and creativity to design worship expressions that fit who you and your church community are.

Let's look at some values and common themes we find in emerging worship gatherings.

1. Emerging worship moves away from a spectator type of gathering

I have been in some worship gatherings where, if you didn't know it was a church, you might think a Broadway play was about to begin. People arrive, are politely greeted at the door, and receive a bulletin as they walk in, much as one receives a playbill program when entering a theater. They walk in the main room and an usher helps them find a seat, again just like a theater. They might have to squeeze down an aisle politely half-smiling at others sitting in that row as they squeeze past them and whisper a polite "excuse me," without stopping to actually talk. They sit in their seat and open the bulletin and read through it like people do in a Broadway theatre, waiting for the "show" to begin. People patiently scan the church bulletin to read the names of the pastoral staff and the outline of the sermon, much as they would read the names of the actors and actresses and scene descriptions in a playbill. They sit and wait until they hear the sounds of instruments being picked up by the worship band, similar to the sounds you would hear when the Broadway orchestra members take their seats and warm up their instruments. This indicates the show is about to begin.

Then the moment everyone is waiting for happens, and the show begins! People look up to the stage and sit as they watch Act I start with the band and band leader cheerfully singing a few songs. Act II includes announcements and promotion about various upcoming church events, much as a theatre company would announce what other plays and events it is doing in the near future. Act III features the main star (the preacher), who comes out and gives a sermon. There is a mix of laughter, emotionally heart-tugging stories, a strong challenge, a surprise twist conclusion, and then a feel-good ending to the message. Everyone claps, the show ends, and then we are dismissed and make our way through the aisles without too much talking to one another apart from the "I really enjoyed that" or "The band was really good this morning" comments about the quality of what they just watched. Out into the parking lot everyone gets into their cars and drives home, holding the playbill bulletin as a token reminder of the event they attended.

I struggled as I wrote these last two paragraphs. I am not trying to demean or mock anyone's church. I love the church deeply and I love worship gatherings, but I have also experienced worship gatherings like the one I just described. I am trying to see if you may have experienced or done any of these things yourself. I know I have been guilty of some of them! It is so easy to subtly shift into making sure that everything runs smoothly, everything is well planned and rehearsed, that our sermons are polished and of high quality. Subtly we begin putting on a "show." Even when our motives and desires are by no means even considering that possibility, it can happen. As we get into the routine of these gatherings weekend after weekend, we can lose sight of the fact that it is not about the production, nor the excellence, nor the way things are programmed, nor how many people are there. It is about coming together to worship God.

What is most frightening to me is that we have subtly trained so many people to view their church experience in this way. We have framed people's expectations of what a worship gathering and church is supposed to be. That is a very sobering thing to ponder. Do people view your "church" as a spectator event? Do they see it as a "show" that they attend once a week and then go home? Have you ever thought about the comments they make as they leave and walk to their cars in the parking lot? Do they say, "The sermon was really good" or "He was really funny this morning" or "I loved that story she told"? Or do they say, "I sensed the Spirit prompting me to do something as a result of how the Scriptures were taught"? There is a big difference between the two.

Nobody intentionally leads worship gatherings with a "show" in mind, but how often it strays in that direction. This happens in contemporary seeker churches, this happens in traditional Baptist churches, this happens in non-denominational Bible churches, and this can happen in emerging churches. If you were honest in the depths of your heart, how much of what I just described are you currently doing in one form or another? I know God works in all kinds of churches, but what I just described goes very much against the emerging values of the emerging church.

Most emerging worship gatherings are trying to do the opposite of what I just described, although we can fall into this just as easily as any other type of church. Ideally, worship gatherings are times for the church community to gather to honor and bring glory to Jesus and worship the King. We may use various worship forms to do this, but it is not a performance or program or show. Let's now take heed to that warning as we get a glimpse of what an emerging worship gathering may look like. Instead of sampling various "shows," let's see worshipers on a mission as they meet together.

2. There is an organic design to the worship gathering

Many emerging worship gatherings seek to be nonlinear. They don't want to be so pre-planned that the Spirit isn't allowed to work in people or change things.

Emerging generations have grown uncomfortable with the boxed-in feel of many contemporary worship services. Instead of a linear design of five songs, a sermon, closing song, and dismissal — emerging worship moves in an organic flow. By organic, I mean the opposite of a rigid pre-set flow that makes the gathering feel like a presentation or performance. Organic means a weaving of many things throughout a meeting that people can participate in. It is much more than just sitting! It is also more than a couple of ways of worshiping.

An organically flowing worship gathering may feature songs, Scripture reading, open sharing, a time of silence, more songs, a message, visuals, and times of quiet and meditation. People may move about the room to stations for prayer, painting, or journaling. Above all, the gathering is participatory.

Being organic is not being unorganized and chaotic. Anything organic and living is the opposite of random. Instead, it has intricate systems developed within it. Human bodies are organic, yet have incredibly interwoven and complex systems to keep the body healthy and growing.

So when I say organic, I'm speaking of a gathering that is carefully planned and prepared. Scripture itself says that "everything" in worship gatherings "should be done in a fitting and orderly way" (1 Corinthians 14:40).

Size does dictate, to some degree, how one designs a worship gathering. When there are 20 to 50 people at a gathering, it is much easier to remain organic and participatory. With a gathering of 500 people, it becomes harder.

Any gathering of more than 100 people takes on a different dynamic. It means thinking through how the greatest number of people can participate. Being organic means intentionally thinking through how not to box things in such a rigid form that it becomes a "presentation" and a "production" instead of a church gathered to worship the risen Jesus. It means thinking through creative ways for more interaction, more involvement than just a sermon and some songs. It may mean setting up enough prayer stations so that everyone can use them, no matter what size the room is. It means changing the setup of the chairs and room to avoid a theater feel. The point of this value is that we are trying to be a family worshiping together, whether we're a group of 10 people in a home or five hundred people in a sanctuary.

> "Therefore, I urge you, brothers, in view of God's mercy, to offer your bodies as living sacrifices, holy and pleasing to God– this is your spiritual act of worship."
> —Romans 12:1

3. A sacred space is created for the worship gathering

Immediately upon entering most emerging worship gatherings, you will notice the attention given to the environment. For gatherings that meet in homes, this isn't always possible, of course, and the home itself is the environment. But in most larger meetings a lot of attention is given to sacred space, whether they meet in a typical church building, a gym, or a storefront shop.

What makes a space visually sacred and conducive to worship, however, is subjective. In many contemporary modern worship settings, well-meaning leaders and designers have removed the sense of awe, wonder, and transcendence. Christians sometimes build and decorate facilities to look like large hotel conference rooms set up for a business presentation.

One church building I visited had 1970s Southern country décor with red- and blue-toned colors and floral wallpaper patterns all around, then asked why younger people visited their church but didn't stick around. Décor is extremely petty and worship is not about the décor. But this church wasn't even in the south—it was in the northwest! It was very uncomfortable aesthetically and way out of sync with emerging generations, who wouldn't see this type of church building as a sacred space for worship.

Emerging generations are very visual. They crave a sense of mystery and wonder of God as they worship. They desire a spiritual environment for worship. That is why in most emerging church gatherings you will see crosses set up on tables or hung or propped up in various other places in the room. In many contemporary and modern churches a large simplistic cross may be displayed behind the pulpit. But emerging churches use crosses, that usually look ancient. Some use Celtic crosses, and some use crosses normally seen in Orthodox churches.

The reason emerging gatherings use crosses is they aren't embarrassed about or hiding the fact that they are gathered to worship the living resurrected Jesus. Many contemporary church buildings have removed the cross or put it off to the side somewhere, but in emerging churches the cross is seen everywhere. They always want to remember that the risen Jesus central is the focus of their gatherings. They also want to aesthetically remind people that Christianity is an ancient faith, prompting their use of Celtic crosses and other artistic and decorative forms of the cross that have more of an ancient feel to them. This is not using the cross as a gimmick; displaying the cross points to Jesus. Even among non-Christians the cross is known as a sacred symbol.

You will see artwork as you walk into emerging worship gatherings. This artwork is displayed all around the room. If the building is theirs to use during the week, you may see murals and artwork that represent the community painted on the walls. You will see artistic prayer stations set up with decorative symbols or props communicating scriptural truths so people can meditate and pray. Bible verses are written in creative ways at these stations and you will see other Scriptures used in artistic ways throughout the emerging worship gathering.

In most emerging worship gatherings, Scripture is seen all around and used in art, at prayer stations, spoken and taught, meditated upon, and used to teach about the meaning of songs that are sung. Usually there is a high reverence and display of Scripture in emerging worship gatherings. Scriptures direct worship, enhance the depth of worship, and are creatively woven throughout a gathering visually and through the spoken word.

In larger gatherings, creativity is used to transform the space through lighting and draping various curtains and dividers. Many times curtains may be used to create pockets of privacy for prayer or to set up prayer stations in certain spaces throughout the room.

Even before the gathering starts, visual images often are projected on screens. Art from throughout the ages, including stained glass artwork, might be shown on the screens to invoke a sense of history and artistry while telling the story of Jesus and stories throughout the Bible. Somewhere in the room there might be artistic props or symbols or paintings displayed that may have something to do with the teaching for that meeting.

The room invokes a sense that this is a spiritual gathering happening here, and that Christianity is not just a modern religion, but an ancient one. The space also communicates loudly that creativity is a vital part of the community culture. This makes a big statement to anyone who visits. Emerging worship expresses love and adoration for God through creativity mixed with theology in artistic expression.

Candles Are Not Just Trendy, But Symbolize the Light of Jesus

The value of worship in emerging worship gatherings is seen in the décor and layout of the room. Usually, candles are used to show the sobriety and seriousness of worship. They also represent the light of Jesus in a dark world. In most emerging worship gatherings, the lighting is dark (not pitch black). The darkness and candles make a beautiful atmosphere where the heart can settle in and focus on worshiping God.

Candles are placed all around the room in order to not focus on the stage. You might see velvet material draped over tables. Remember, Christianity is highly criticized for being a modern, contemporary, organized religion. Therefore, the more we show the Christian faith's ancient roots and history, the more emerging generations will be free to worship.

Candles are not trendy since they have been symbols used in churches throughout history. People have symbolically lit candles when saying a prayer in many traditional churches. What is sad is that most evangelical contemporary churches have removed candles, so when candles are used now in emerging worship they are often dismissed as trendy. Yet the very people who criticize candles often use them in their churches on Christmas Eve, on New Year's Eve, and at weddings.

A Living Room-Like Feel, Even if 500 People Are There

A living room setting is a common theme in worship rooms. This is done in the hope of avoiding any sense of a theater feeling. Instead, the goal is to promote community and a sense of family. Solomon's Porch, an emerging church in Minneapolis, has set up their meeting room with couches and chairs for several hundred people. The way they speak, and the way the meeting functions, is very much like a large living room. When people speak, it is generally from the middle with people all around.

Most emerging worship gatherings have moved past the rows-of-chairs-facing-the-stage environment because of their values. Even if there is a stage of sorts, the chairs are usually set up wrapping around it in more of a community feel than in straight rows. Even churches that have pews usually add chairs and create spaces around the room for people to move to so they are not in pews the whole time. Some meetings may set up round tables as a seating option. Setting up tables communicates that this is more than just a theater-like meeting with rows all facing the stage.

You Probably Pay More Attention to Your "Space" than You Think

You may think it is silly paying all this attention to the aesthetic "space" for a worship gathering. True, we can worship anywhere, and worship is not about us. If Christianity was persecuted in America and the church was in hiding, we wouldn't care if we met in a cave or barn. But the fact is that today, for most people, aesthetics do matter. It probably matters to you, too. Even if you used a rented space, you probably bring in décor to communicate something and help set the atmosphere. This doesn't need to be blown out of proportion, but it is important.

The Scriptures have graphic portrayals of color, space, and action in worship in both the Old and New Testaments. In Revelation 4, for instance, the language invokes emotion and mood by its aesthetic description of God's throne in heaven. This all needs to be in balance and perspective, but let's not ignore the fact that values do change our aesthetics for our worship space.

4. A multisensory approach to the worship gathering

Multisensory worship involves seeing, hearing, tasting, smelling, touching, and experiencing. This means our worship of God can involve singing, silence, preaching, and art, and move into a much greater spectrum of expression. It goes outside the box and then throws away the box that limits how we can express our love and worship to God when we gather. We move past merely listening and singing to a whole new level of ways to participate in worship through all our senses.

Some emerging worship gatherings choose to be very reflective when people walk in and start with personal prayer and quiet reflection. They may do this all the time or when the gathering is specially designed to begin in this manner. During this reflective time, instructions and Scriptures might be projected on the screens to encourage people to take time to quiet their hearts.

Quite often throughout the worship gathering there will be pauses for prayer. Prayers may take place during the sermon and the musical worship. Prayers may be read together. Times may be given for people to pray in silence. Prayer may continue in small groups and privately after the gathering. Prayer is threaded throughout the gathering, not simply tagged on at the beginning or end of the sermon.

Going back to a New Testament practice, many emerging worship gatherings have a meal together before the actual formal gathering starts to further enhance their sense of community. Meals are becoming a big part of the community aspect of emerging worship, and it shouldn't surprise us since meals were so common in the early church. Larger gatherings may try to have communal meals once a month or before the meeting starts. But there is an interesting rising value of family-style meals as part of emerging worship. Virtually all emerging worship gatherings have reinstated the Passover Seder meal as part of their calendar year of worship.

There Are Leaders – But It Makes a Big Difference How One Leads

In most emerging worship gatherings, you'll sing uplifting songs of praise and singing to start the meeting, but this singing feels more communal. It's not a singalong with someone up front leading. Much of this communal feel has to do with who is leading, how he or she is leading, and where he or she is leading from. Leading worship or speaking from a raised stage is much different than leading and speaking from among the people.

There is a brutal attempt in most emerging worship gatherings to not have "leaders" draw attention themselves as they lead during the meeting. The organic tone is communal, so there's a sense of everyone being equals. There are no "stars" at any gathering. The worship leader and band may be positioned in the rear or on the side of the room so the spotlight is not on them. The worship leader and band may even lead from among the people if the room allows, so everyone can be together. The lighting may be done in a way where the band is covered in shadows so the attention is not on them. The focus is on Jesus and on the worship itself, not on profiling singers or spotlighting the band and making them the direct center of attention during worship.

Eclectic Styles of Music Are Very Common in Emerging Worship

Musical worship styles are usually a reflection of a specific community. Most emerging worship gatherings are moving beyond Christian-pop and moving into a post-Matt Redman form of musical worship combining the ancient with pop rhythms, global music, and other forms of eclectic and ambient music. An emerging worship gathering in the city of Chicago fuses hip-hop with the ancient and with pop. An emerging worship gathering in Minnesota focuses primarily on songs the community writes and is more folk-sounding.

In Vintage Faith Church, we use an eclectic blend of the ancient with contemporary pop. We have even formed a choir to sing ancient choral songs and Taizé- style chants fused with contemporary pop. (Taizé is an international, ecumenical community in France that uses simple, scripturally-based meditative singing in worship.) We are using the choir to back the worship band and provide meditative songs for prayer.

I imagine choirs becoming a big part of emerging worship. I'm not talking about the rather corny 1970s and '80s style of Christian choir music. Instead, I see choirs that go back and study ancient choral music and also sing gospel spirituals and other choir music that invokes both reverence and joy. If there is a choir, they will not sing from a stage all wearing the same color sweaters, all smiling with lots of make-up. The choir is off to the side or in the back, out of sight, and out of the spotlight, so their voices are what's noticed.

Music is not categorized in emerging church worship since it is a reflection of the church community and not simply repeating whatever top ten worship songs are playing on Christian radio stations. DJs with turntables are sometimes used in the band adding layers of sound and rhythm to the worship music. Many times ambient music is played for reflection during worship. There is some global music influence and definitely an eclectic feel to the worship music during a gathering.

What the music is like depends on the particular community. Many emerging worship gatherings write their own worship music more and more to further reflect their unique local community expressions of adoration and praise.

You Will Probably See Art and Visuals Used as an Expression of Worship

During community singing at the beginning of a gathering, lots of visuals may be on the screens. Those visuals may include still images, video clips of symbols, and other looping images. There may be a sequence of images of the cross, with all types of crosses being shown, reminding people that the reason they are there is to remember and focus on the risen Jesus. There may be a series of images of space, planets, and solar systems, reminding people of the fact that God is creator of all things and the stars and heavens reflect his handiwork. There may be images of church building exteriors and interiors from Europe, which are extremely beautiful and cause people to reflect on the fact that God is transcendent and we are here to meet with him.

Many times the art has been created by individuals in the community, reflecting who the local gathering is. You may see art from throughout church history, including artwork by Michelangelo, Gustave Doré, and other masters. You might see global expressions of Christian art from different cultures. You may see abstract images of art from contemporary times. You might see photography from those in the local church body, or photography that reflects the personality and culture of the local worship gathering. One thing you won't see is cheesy Christian art! I know "cheesy" is subjective, but emerging worship gatherings are pretty sensitive to reflect culturally what will resonate with emerging generations. There is little tolerance for anything that is corny or Christian-eesy. (Again, I know this is subjective, but I think you know what I mean!)

Artistic Expressions in Worship

As we have already mentioned, emerging worship gatherings use a multisensory approach to the creation of a sacred space. Art is used to help create a sense of space, but it also is used as an expression of worship. The opportunity is given for people to paint, to draw, and to write poetry during a worship gathering. This often occurs during a prolonged musical set of worship after a message. Tables and prayer stations for art worship may be set up around the room. Sometimes there are tables covered with butcher paper so people can draw or write out prayers as an expression of worship. Children who participate in worship gatherings are able to draw at tables like this. Sometimes there may be actual art stations set up where one can go and have the freedom to paint an expression of his or her worship during the message or singing. At other stations people can use clay to create sculpture as an expression of worship. Sometimes the art is of Jesus' face or the cross. Many times the art is more abstract in content, but is heartfelt in expressing the worship they have for God. Art is also digitally displayed on video screens during the worship gathering. This often includes a mixture of art that individuals in the church have produced and a plethora of Christian art down through the ages. This projected art may be used as backdrops to Scriptures, songs, words used in sermons, or recited prayers. Artwork may be left up on the screens for long or short periods of time during the gathering. Projected art can include video images and looping photos of candles, crosses, or nature scenes.

At a Youth Specialties convention, three sets of black and white images of ancient church interiors and exteriors were projected simultaneously during the meetings. These images of beautiful church architecture created a worship space in a very large, modern convention hall.

Incense can be used to awaken the senses and direct attention to the way prayers

"A stage is a dangerous place to be, because a stage is a raised platform. Stages are built so that little people can be seen more easily by larger audiences. The lights are bright. The sound is big. Yet if we are not careful, those of us who lead worship can allow the stage to succeed, making more of us than we really are."
—Louie Giglio

ascend before the throne of God. We also use incense when discussing how financial giving is an offering that goes up before the throne. Candles may also have a worshipful aroma associated with them.

One worship gathering baked bread inside the room before the gathering began. This was meant to evoke a sense of hunger when people walked into the room. The theme of that particular meeting was hungering for God and Jesus as the bread of life.

During the message, speakers incorporate art images into their teaching. Art is sometimes used to provoke thinking through the display of specific images and symbols. Large props may be built and used for teaching.

We recently presented a series on the portrait of a disciple. Several individuals in the church painted huge eight-foot paintings of a hand, a heart, and a head. These tied directly into the series theme about being followers of Jesus with our hands, hearts, and heads. The art visuals were displayed throughout the series and then hung on the walls when the series ended.

Prayer stations are a great way to invoke the senses and express worship. Generally people move to the prayer stations during a prolonged time of musical worship after a message is given. People roam about the room and interact in prayer. Prayer stations are usually tables set up on the outskirts of the room. They have fabric draped over them with interactive themes usually based on that day's teaching. They might have curtains enclosing them for privacy. They usually have Scripture creatively written so people can stop, read, and meditate on the Word of God. They might have cards to write out prayers and place them in baskets.

At a prayer station, the sense of touch can be experienced. One station may have bowls of sand for people to run their fingers through in order to remind them of the teaching they just heard in which the imagery of sand was used to described being dry and thirsty for God.

Salt packets may be left at prayer stations so people can taste it and read what Jesus said in Matthew 5:13 about being salt. People could put pins on a world map in specific countries as they pray for them. A fresh vine and a dry vine can be set up to show the contrast Jesus used in John 15.

Bowls of water to wash one's hands in may be set on tables to communicate how clean and pure we are washed by the blood of Jesus. Some stations may allow prayers to be written out. Other stations may have molding clay to express a prayer.

Sermons Are Invitations into Kingdom Living by Telling the Story

"Hearing" is an important part of worship. Sermons may be delivered, but again, the format of how a sermon or teaching is given depends on the size of the gathering. Some emerging worship gatherings choose to not have sermons or to have only short sermons and times of teaching. This isn't because they don't value the teaching of the Scriptures, but because they have chosen to focus their teaching of the Scriptures in more interactive ways in other settings (classes, homes, discussion groups), which is actually more in tune with how emerging generations best learn something.

Some emerging worship gatherings, including some in England, take this further and rarely have preaching or even pop-rock worship bands. Instead, they may simply have ambient music playing in the background. Their gatherings primarily consist of people going to creative stations to pray, read Scripture, and meditate, plus some communal readings together.

Most emerging worship gatherings, however, have someone who preaches anywhere from as little as 15 minutes to as many as 50 minutes. But the preaching is not with a I-am-the-wise-one-with-the-answers-from-the-Bible-because-I-went-to-seminary-and-am-giving-it-to-you-now-because-I-have-the-microphone-and-the-power-so-you-need-to-listen attitude. Instead, their messages are presented as a humble exploration and teaching of the Scriptures.

Emerging preachers see themselves as fellow journeyers. Preaching is no longer an authoritative transferring of biblical information. Instead, it's becoming more about spiritual formation and Kingdom living. As pastor and author Brian McLaren says about emerging worship preaching, "The preacher becomes the leader of a kind of group meditation, less scholar and more sage, less lecturer and more poet, prophet, and priest."

In many emerging worship gatherings there is an attempt to dialogue as much as possible with the people in the gathering, but the larger the gathering the harder it is for a preacher to truly interact and dialogue with others while preaching. Still, there can be planned or spontaneous occasions for open mic or open sharing despite the size of the group, even if it numbers in the hundreds.

No matter what size group, in emerging worship the sermon is more of an invitation into Kingdom living rather than focused on the five steps for this or that wrapped up with clean application points. Sermons are applicable by their nature if we're speaking about Kingdom living as a disciple, but the emerging approach to sermons is telling the "story of God" and inviting others into that story instead of outlining propositional principles out of the Bible and turning them into sermon application points.

Interestingly, when you study the origin of our current forms of preaching taught in most seminaries, what we have been doing in most churches does not find its origin in Scripture. Most of our contemporary forms of preaching were derived from fifth century BCE Greek sophists (i.e., Greek teachers credited with inventing the art of persuasive speaking known as rhetoric). Aristotle (384-322 BCE), for instance, developed the three-point speech. After Christianity spread into the Mediterranean areas, the Greco-Roman influence shaped how Christian leaders taught. Historical church leaders such as John Chrysostom (AD 347-407) and Augustine (AD 354-430) dramatically changed how preaching was seen and made the oratory forms of the Greek and Latin styles the model for church sermons.

I'm giving this brief explanation of the origin of the way we preach today in order to stress that the emerging church is beginning to change forms of preaching, but that doesn't mean we are straying from the Scriptures! It is simply teaching and preaching using different forms of communication. Scripture is not neglected at all. Instead, it is raised all the higher in the emerging church.

Many times the message in an emerging worship gathering is broken into parts. Instead of one long sermon, you'll see the interaction of song or communal reciting of prayers in between sections of the sermon. Some emerging worship gatherings may allow people to actually get up and move to art stations to paint or draw or sculpt clay during the sermon. That way, as they listen, they can create art that expresses what they are hearing.

The messages in gatherings use a lot of humor. They're full of life and laughter and can be intensely passionate and convicting. At the same time, they reflect seriousness and humility because they are presented by a fellow worshiper struggling along in life like everyone else. The Scriptures are taught in larger chunks of verses and chapters and there's even a strong emphasis on walking through books of the Bible rather than simply pulling in one verse from here and there.

Quite often the historical Jewish roots of the Christian faith are examined to bring the Scriptures to life in their original settings. I don't think that most emerging church worship gatherings can be criticized for watering down Scripture or not using it. If anything, there is a resurgence and respect for the Scriptures. In fact, the Scriptures have been brought back into the forefront. Emerging sermons are not just someone's opinion about a theme plus a quick verse or two tossed in for good measure.

The Scriptures are the ancient and living Word that the emerging church grapples with and wrestles with and turns to for guidance and light.

5. Freedom of movement in worship

In most emerging worship gatherings, people aren't forced to remain stationary in their seats for the whole meeting. There is no rush out the door after a message ends, either.

Music is a big part of how one slows down to allow the Spirit to speak. The influence of Taizé, the international ecumenical community in France where thousands of European post-Christians go each summer, has helped influence the revival of ancient Christian music, which many emerging churches incorporate with modern elements. Taizé worship is extremely meditative, often using only a few words repeated several times, so the worshiper can both pray and listen to God as he or she sings.

During this time of more reflective worship, people are allowed to leave their seats and go to prayer stations around the room. Prayer stations are spaces created in the room for people to use to help guide them in prayer and many times have interactive elements as part of them. They usually have Scriptures written out to guide people in prayer about various things that may tie into what was taught in the sermon. During these times of contemplative musical worship, people feel the freedom to leave their seats and go kneel down or lie on their faces to pray and communicate to God. They have the freedom to leave their seats and go to community journals at prayer stations set up for people to write out prayers and thoughts. There might be places set up where they can paint and or artistically express worship using other materials.

It is common for people to leave their seats during the musical worship, which can last for 20 or 30 minutes. A few churches even encourage people to move about and experience different things in the worship space during the preaching.

Having the freedom to move about at appropriate times during the worship gathering is a very freeing and beautiful thing in emerging worship. People are free to pray on their own, pray with others, or go to a prayer, art, or journaling station while musical worship plays.

During a gathering some people may still sit, and some people may move about quite a bit. The point is, there is freedom depending upon where someone is at and how the Spirit may be working in his or her life.

Someone may need to pray with a brother or sister in Christ. Another person may need to be on his or her face, praying in repentance. Someone may choose to kneel as a sign of submission. Others may want to stand.

6. A different focal point

No matter how the preaching and teaching occurs in an emerging worship gathering, the focus is not on building a one- or two-person show.

The preaching usually does not occur from an elevated stage. As the size of the room permits, it may take place in the midst of the people instead of above them on a stage. If it is a large group meeting, the stage may be extended into the people as much as possible. There is a plurality of people in the church involved in reading Scripture passages, sharing poems, and participating in other ways so the focus is not always on one person.

During the sermon, artwork, props, and symbols are often used to communicate the message. It's interesting that in most youth and children's ministries we use props to communicate, but when we speak to adults we don't use them. Yet in Scripture you see Jesus referring to things there near him, including a fig tree in Matthew 21:18-22, to make a point. Communicating with visuals is very much part of emerging worship gatherings.

Even if there is one primary teacher in a local church, the speaking is shared as much as possible. The desire is to avoid developing a dependency upon one person in the worship gathering (or a dependency on a certain personality or style of teaching).

Interestingly, teaching in the synagogues and home churches in biblical times was a shared responsibility. Often, several individuals would teach in a given gathering. Jesus and the apostle Paul were invited to be guest teachers in many cities. Typically, though, the teachers lived in the local community. There were no elevated platforms for teachers to stand above people.

This value is reflected in having an extended stage that goes "among" the people — even in gatherings with hundreds of people. The preacher is not seen as above or separate from the congregation, but among them.

When the church began adopting public speaking rhetorical skills from Greek culture, the modern sermon as we know it began to form. The focus shifted to the oration skills of a single person rather than the participatory teaching first developed in synagogues and home churches.

Then when Constantine erected the first church buildings (after AD 327), preaching changed again. Sermons in these new buildings were first delivered from chairs. John Chrysostom (AD 347-407) moved the focus of preaching to an *ambo*, a raised desk from which sermons were delivered. The pulpit came soon after that ("pulpit" is derived from the Latin word *pulpitum*, which means "stage"). The pulpit was put in the highest and most visible place for all to see.

All of this was in contrast to the practices of the early church.

In emerging church worship gatherings, the teaching and preaching spring from the community. Jesus is the centerpiece, not the preacher.

This also applies to musical leaders and worship bands. Emerging worship is not a pop concert and the leader of musical worship needs to reflect this in his or her approach to leading. We are moving away from flashy colored lights focusing on the band. Instead, the musical worship leader and the band are trying to disappear rather than be staring out at everyone. It is rather odd, after all, for worship bands commissioned to lead others in worship of God to stand center stage with all the lights and attention on them. In emerging worship, the band may be off to the side, out of center stage, or mixed in with the people if the room is small enough. In our setting we set up the band in the rear of the room as often as possible so as to not draw undue attention to them.

The communal reading of creeds, prayers, and Scriptures also enhance the sense of community. Usually a small team (both sexes represented) work together to lead a worship gathering. Individuals may present Scripture recitations, poetry readings, and prayers, but everything has a clear community orientation instead of focusing on only one or two individuals.

7. A revival of liturgy, ancient disciplines, Christian seasons, and Jewish roots

In many modern contemporary churches we have basically ignored the historical church's practices of worship. The ironic thing is that, among emerging generations, there is a desire to seek the ancient. There is even a backlash against the church feeling like a modern business. So a revival of liturgy and other ancient disciplines, when brought back with life and meaning, are a desired approach to worship in the emerging church. I'm not suggesting we abandon all contemporary forms of worship and music. I'm simply suggesting we don't ignore 2,000 years of church history. There are beautiful expressions of worship from various time periods we can integrate into how we worship today.

Depending on the denomination and history of your church, liturgy may or may not be included in your church background. Liturgy is more than the use of incense and other rituals often associated with the word. The word "liturgy" originally meant a "public work" or a "service in the name of or on behalf of the people." In Christian tradition, it means the participation of the people of God in "the work of God."

In *Introduction to Christian Worship,* James F. White says liturgy "is the quintessence of the priesthood of the believers that the whole priestly community of Christians shares. To call a service 'liturgical' is to indicate that it was conceived so that all worshipers take an active part in offering their worship together."

Church history shows liturgy's development through the ages and how it came to designate the church's rituals and practices in worship gatherings. This includes communion and baptism in almost every branch of the church. In Roman Catholic, Eastern Orthodox, and Anglican churches, you'll find a well-developed calendar and more set pattern of worship. In many American branches of the church, however, liturgical practices were removed and forgotten a long time ago. Yet among emerging generations there is a desire to embrace Christianity's ancient forms of worship, which include liturgy.

In the book *Soul Shaper,* Tony Jones explains a lot of ancient spiritual disciples and shows how they can be attractive ways of worship for emerging generations. *Lectio divina*, which is the practice of repeatedly meditating and praying through a passage of Scripture, and many other spiritual exercises are being reintroduced in emerging worship gatherings.

There also is a growing practice in emerging worship to focus on the Christian calendar, which is organized around two major seasons of sacred time: Advent, Christmas, and Epiphany; and Lent, Holy Week, Easter, and Pentecost. Churches that have used liturgy for some time are breathing new life into their "routine" practices. Other emerging worship gatherings are revising ancient practices.

This movement into ancient forms of worship includes a revival of understanding and teaching about the Jewish roots of the faith. Most emerging churches include a Passover Seder as part of their worship year. They spend considerable time teaching the Jewish perspective of the Bible.

Interestingly, among emerging generations there is a fascinating revival of interest in singing hymns as part of worship. The lyrical content of many hymns is rich and deep, something emerging generations desire. The fact that we can become part of the church's story by singing songs that are hundreds of years old demonstrates that

Christianity is not a modern religion, but has deep historic roots. Some nineteenth and twentieth century lyrics are steeped in modernity, but many beautiful ancient hymns are worth including in emerging worship.

There is also a growing passion for emerging churches to write their own songs of worship. This way musical worship is all the more reflective of the local church itself.

8. An emphasis on prayer

Another common theme woven throughout emerging worship gatherings is the elevation of prayer. Plenty of time is given for people to slow down, quiet their hearts, and then pray at various stations and with others.

There is a strong focus on allowing time for quiet contemplation in emerging worship gatherings. Not that it's all somber—there are great times of upbeat celebration and energy. But it's too easy to fail to take enough time to quiet our hearts and ask God's Spirit to lead and prompt us.

We need to allow the Spirit to convict or encourage our hearts after a message — rather than rush out the door. We need times where we can intercede for others or get on our knees to confess our sins.

9. Communion as a central part of emerging worship

Communion is a central part of worship in most emerging worship gatherings. Many take communion weekly, but not in a nonchalant or routine manner!

Before the Reformation, the Eucharist was central to worship. In many modern churches today, communion has turned so predictable that it has lost its beauty. The wonder of worship and remembering what Jesus did has faded away.

There is a rising longing among emerging generations for the Lord's Supper to once again be a central part of worship. It is usually a major part of the gathering—a time for people to quiet their hearts, reflect, pray, confess sin, and offer words of thanksgiving. Most emerging worship gatherings set up communion so people must walk to receive it.

Our church once laid a very large cross down flat on a series of tables. The entire cross was lit with candles on top so the cross's shape glowed. The communion elements were put all around the cross on the tables it lay on. People came forward to the cross to receive the elements.

Like the early church, some emerging gatherings have made communion part of a meal. The best guess is that the bread and cup weren't separated from the meal until the time of Tertullian (AD 160-225).

However it is done, the Lord's Supper is a core practice in emerging worship gatherings.

10. Jesus as the centerpiece of worship

The most refreshing value of emerging worship gatherings is the focus on practicing the presence of Jesus in everything.

To be blunt, many modern contemporary worship services are more anthropocentric than Christocentric. Jesus' name is mentioned here and there, yet he is almost a side issue to the real focus: learning basic principles about living a better life.

Emerging worship gatherings leave no doubt that Jesus is the centerpiece of the gathering. This is true of the prayers, the symbols of the cross, and the deemphasis of the preacher and musical worship leader.

It's also true of the messages, which focus on being a follower of Jesus and true Kingdom living (which Jesus talked about so much).

Remember...

Emerging worship is not one specific approach to worship. You'll find many of these ten values in various emerging worship gatherings, including the ones we'll see in Part 2. But each local body is distinct and different. All emerging worship gatherings practice some of these values—and some gatherings practice all of them.

You may wonder how you can possibly incorporate all of these values into your worship gathering. Just selecting the music and coming up with a new sermon every week is hard enough! The next chapter shows ways to begin designing emerging worship gatherings.

Emerging Thoughts

1. Did any of these 10 values surprise you?

2. Would you be interested in studying the history of worship gatherings in order to explore where the sermon, pulpit, steeple, and buildings came from? If so, what practice in your church would you like to study?

3. Of the 10 values described above, which do you see as strengths in your church? Which ones do you want to think about or focus on in the months ahead?

CHAPTER 8

Planning and Creating Multi-Sensory Worship Gatherings

But we must listen carefully to this generation and reread Scripture in the light of their dreams and fears. Then perhaps we will present the gospel and plan our worship in ways that respond to their quest and reintegrate words and image. It is possible that we might actually win the battle of words but lose the battle of images. And losing that battle could well cost us this generation.

—William Dyrness,
Visual Faith

Virtually every time I speak with church leaders about incorporating multi-sensory elements in their worship gatherings, the reaction is predictable. I immediately hear responses such as:

- "We can never do this. It must take tons of staff to pull this off. Our team is almost all volunteers!"
- "This must cost so much money. As a small church, we can't afford to do this."

- "I can't imagine doing this every week. It would wipe us out!"
- "Are you saying we aren't going to be successful if we don't use multisensory elements in worship every weekend? If so, I'm depressed!"
- "Our senior pastor doesn't tell us what he is preaching on until the week before!"
- "How can we be creative like this if our pastor doesn't plan ahead?"

These are very valid questions and concerns.

Moving into the more multisensory approach of emerging worship does mean shifting how we do things. It does take more effort. So much depends on your individual church situation. You don't have to change everything overnight. It takes time!

Let's look at a few ways you can begin implementing some emerging forms of worship in your church.

Multisensory Worship Gatherings Don't Have to Happen Every Week!

It can feel overwhelming to think of creating prayer stations, adding art, setting up a sacred space, and planning other elements of an emerging gathering every week. Especially if you have a small staff or no paid staff. You don't have to start doing something every week. How often you meet for a multisensory gathering depends on your local situation.

Some emerging churches have enough staff and volunteer teams to design and create something on a weekly basis. As long as they are focusing on the non-gathering aspects of spiritual formation and aren't creating consumer-Christians, this is great!

The big danger is wiping out your staff and volunteers by putting too much focus on the weekend gathering. Save 80 percent of your energy for home churches and other midweek aspects of spiritual formation.

House Churches That Gather Together Once a Month

There are some emerging churches that are fully composed of house churches that meet weekly in homes for worship. They get together in one larger gathering only once a month. This is a great chance for them to have a very creative and multisensory worship experience together as a larger community.

Monthly Special Alternative Worship Gatherings

Westwinds Church in Jackson, Michigan, has creative worship gatherings every Sunday, but they go all-out with full multisensory worship only one evening a month.

Once, they built a temporary 30-foot by 20-foot wide pond out of large plastic sheets and stones inside their worship center. During this gathering, people could say a prayer, light a candle, and send it out across the pond.

Another time they spread sand across the floor to communicate the meaning of being in a desert experience. They talked about what can be learned from times of dryness in one's spiritual life.

One evening their topic was forgiveness, so they encouraged people to drop pebbles into 55-gallon drums full of water. People watched the pebbles disappear into the black nothingness at the bottom, which represented their sins disappearing because of God's forgiveness.

Glass bottles half filled with water were poured out on a huge rock set up in the center of the auditorium to represent the theme of pouring out our lives as drink offerings (Philippians 2:17 and 2 Timothy 4:6).

These certainly made powerful and memorable evenings of worship. But they are not something that can be done weekly in most churches, so Westwind plans more extreme worship once a month. This is our approach in Vintage Faith Church.

Making Small but Consistent Changes

The staff at one church in rural Oklahoma had read about multisensory worship. They fully believed they needed to start making changes in the way they worshiped in order to be in line with the emerging culture and emerging generations. Instinctively, everything in them knew that they needed to approach worship in a more holistic manner by incorporating visuals and the senses.

These staff members were afraid, however, to try anything too radical. After all, they served in a very conservative Baptist church. One staff member told me he thought that as soon as they lit one candle, the congregation would complain and mistrust would develop.

Still, they knew they had to do something. At first, they started by slowly adding a few things to their youth meetings. They corporately read ancient creeds and prayers. They lit candles and had times of silent prayer. They allowed the youth to paint during a worship time. They practiced *lectio divina* or "sacred reading," the ancient practice of prayerful meditation on Scripture. Not all at once, but little by little they added these elements of worship to their existing meetings. Most of the youth loved worshiping God this way. It renewed a passion for worship among them!

Remember, this youth group had never done anything like this. It was a huge step for them. The response with the youth was so great that the staff are planning to have monthly emerging worship gatherings for the youth (and adults of any age who want to come). Non-believers who weren't interested in the other Sunday morning services at this church are now interested in being part of the new gathering. Eventually the church wants to turn the monthly worship gathering into a weekly one.

Depending on your church situation, you can start implementing a new monthly or weekly worship gathering. Or you can begin by making changes to your existing worship service. Whatever you do, make sure people know the why behind what you're doing so it doesn't seem like a new fad. Worship is not a gimmick. Worship is going before a holy God and expressing our love for him. The form of our worship may change, but the God we worship does not!

> "When worship is the subject, little leaders are what we need. I don't necessarily mean small in stature but small in terms of self, for there is no other enemy of true worship besides self."
> —Louie Giglio

Worship Is Not about Being Multisensory

Worship is not about being multisensory, but about worshiping God! These are just ideas of how emerging generations are beginning to connect in community worship.

The implementation of a multisensory worship gathering is only one small part of your church's spiritual formation and experience. The weekend worship gathering and the effort we put into it must be put into perspective of the holistic life of the church. Remember, we do not want to build on the foundation of the worship gathering, but on Jesus and the mission he gave us.

Emerging Worship Gatherings Involve Community Planning

If you want to start a new multisensory worship gathering or make changes to what you do now, involve people in your church or youth ministry.

I am always amazed at pastors and other staff members who work in isolation to create worship gatherings. The senior pastor preps a sermon. The worship pastor or worship leader preps the songs. Then they present what they prepared to the congregation, which receives it. This is not a good trait for any type of worship gathering. It especially goes against the values of emerging church worship. We want to allow people to worship, free of the weight of what happens in the worship gathering, but team planning is essential.

If you want to move to a multisensory approach, create a large team — a community — to plan and design these gatherings. This will turn your worship from highly controlled, linear "shows" for consumers to colorful community-owned gatherings involving many voices, hearts, and minds. Multisensory is not "solo-sensory" or "one-dimensional sensory."

Let's explore what this means.

The Old Paradigm of Worship-Service Planning

Typically, the senior pastor determines in isolation what happens in a weekend service. The pastor usually selects (with prayer) the message he will preach.

Since preaching in the contemporary modern church is the centerpiece of the worship service, the song selection and anything else added to the sermon is simply extra. Worship leaders generally wait on the senior pastor to tell them what is happening so they can select songs. If there's time, a drama or another creative "extra" might be thrown in.

Even in large megachurches with multiple staff, worship pastors, and leaders must wait on the senior pastor to let them know his plans for the weekend. Sometimes it's Wednesday or Thursday when he finally gives enough direction to the worship leader for creative planning to begin.

Let's look at this a different way.

Shifting Values of Worship Planning

MODERN	EMERGING
The senior pastor determines what is taught in the worship services	The lead pastor involves both the church community and the staff in determining what is taught in the worship gatherings
The sermon is the center of the worship service — music and anything else are "extra"	The combination of many creative elements experienced in community points to Jesus as the centerpiece
The senior pastor gives the worship leader direction for enhancing the sermon with music and other creative elements	The worship team (including the lead pastor) direct the design of the worship gatherings
The weekend service team consists of the senior pastor and worship leader alone	The weekend service team includes the teacher, the musical leader, the artists, the photographers, the video and PowerPoint team, the sacred space team, etc.
Creativity causes stress to the pastors who own it. They must always outdo what they did last time in order to please people	Creativity causes relief and lack of stress as worship gatherings become more fluid, more naturally creative, thanks to the efforts of a team of people

Emerging Worship Planning in Community

"So here I am in the place of worship, eyes open, drinking in your strength and glory."
—Psalm 63:2
(The Message)

In *The Emerging Church*, I spoke of the way leadership is moving from a hierarchical top-down style to a team-based, interconnected, empowering style. The same is true of worship teams. The chart above reflects some of the changing values of planning emerging worship gatherings in community.

The good news is that you don't need a big staff or big budget. Many churches do this with no staff and a minimal budget. However, it does require building a worship community and advance planning.

Here are some suggestions of how to think about planning emerging worship with a team.

1. Start with the community to determine what Scriptures and themes should be taught

Begin by constantly talking with the people in the church community itself. What are their dreams, their hurts, and their struggles? Invite them to write and turn in their prayer requests, which will reveal a lot about the church and the needs of the people.

Beside their needs, what are the things of God and Scripture that people need to know? As a leader, you may need to teach things they normally wouldn't ask for. Charles Spurgeon, a renowned London preacher in the 1800s, equated choosing what we preach to a doctor choosing medicine for a patient.

As leaders, we must know the people of our church. We can't write out random prescriptions and expect people to be "healed." We cannot allow ourselves to become disconnected from the people of our church, even if it's a large community. Spending time with a select number of people will not give us an accurate view of the whole church's thoughts and needs.

We can correspond with our key leaders via e-mail or in meetings. As shepherds, they hear and know the people of the church better than anyone. Ask them for suggestions on what teaching needs to occur in the worship gatherings.

As you listen, above all, be in prayer and ask God to lead you in your preaching.

2. Involve the staff in the process

After we collect insights from people in your church, we can meet with the other pastors and staff of your church. Many pastors are the only paid staff their church has and don't have this privilege. If you do, it is a powerful thing to plan worship services with other people. For example, the youth pastor may have tremendous insights into what the whole church may need to learn in the worship service. Don't leave him feeling isolated from what goes on in the worship gatherings.

Involving staff in sermon planning is a wonderful way to incorporate their input and show the team's value. Instead of the senior or lead pastor telling the staff, "Here's what is happening," the senior or lead pastor should ask their staff, "What do you sense we should teach?"

Discuss the insights the staff gleans from the people of the church. Then discuss the insights you have gleaned. Constantly bathe this whole process in prayer.

3. Determine the teaching topics or theme at least two months in advance

After we have received insight from the community and staff, we now need to seek God as a priority. We need to discern where he wants our church to go in terms of the preaching and teaching in the weekend worship gatherings. This is a huge responsibility (as all teaching is) and should be done on our knees.

Don't neglect to pray as you select a book of the Bible to walk through or schedule another type of thematic teaching series. Whoever is responsible for determining the preaching and teaching should lay out a schedule at least two or three months in advance. When a church is on top of things, it should plan the basic themes of the worship gatherings six to 12 months in advance. Imagine the creativity you could unleash by doing that and having the margin to plan ahead.

If you are designing multisensory worship gatherings, advance planning is critically important. The planning can be general in terms of what topics you will teach or what Scriptures you will use. The title of the series should be determined, as well. If you follow a liturgical calendar, this is easy since it is already laid out for you. When this is done in advance, your worship teams can thoughtfully design worship gatherings with Jesus at the very center.

This doesn't mean we stick to our preplanned calendar when the Spirit of God shifts things around. There is also a need to be flexible when something in the church dictates the need for a specific teaching. The key is to be flexible and organic in planning. Things may change as the Spirit directs. But we can at least be prepared in advance and pray to see if God wants anything different as we go.

Each message and series should be carefully tied into the church's mission and values. This will help you be wise in what you do in your worship gatherings. Of course, you are doing worship! But just as Jesus taught different things in different seasons of the Jewish year and took advantage of the metaphors of life wherever he traveled, we should take advantage of our calendar year and the flow of life that people in our community experience.

4. Develop metaphors and themes from the Scriptures

I believe we should develop movement and direction in our weekend worship gatherings. If you teach through a book of the Bible, you can still develop themes from it. If you follow the liturgical calendar, you can still create a theme or metaphor to use. You can also break down sections of a book of the Bible into a mini-series. We started Vintage Faith Church by going through the Sermon on the Mount and breaking it down into three mini-series over four months. I believe it is a beneficial thing to design teaching series that last three to six weeks. This way they can create a sense of direction and momentum.

I am not suggesting that we use felt-need marketing principles in emerging worship. I have seen great enthusiasm develop in weekend worship gatherings, however, when the title is given to a series we are beginning. If you have a monthly emerging worship gathering, you may still give it a thematic title and design what is done around that theme. An alternative worship gathering called Grace that meets once a month in London gives each of their monthly gatherings a name: "Wonder," "Homecoming," "Fire," "I am the Way," "Promised Land," or "1+1 + 1 = 1." Each of these evenings focuses on Jesus through multisensory worship using that evening's specific theme.

5. Design worship services in community

All the leaders involved in your worship gathering, staff and volunteers, should meet on a regular basis. How frequently your worship gathering takes place will determine how often your team needs to meet.

You may want to meet every month for half a day to plan out the next month. This gives you a longer time together to pray and think through ideas. If you choose to do this, you should still have weekly reviews of the previous worship gathering and time to look ahead for the next week's gathering.

The goal is to put the design of your emerging worship gatherings into the hands of many people — not just one or two.

I suggest that you form a leadership team made up of everyone who leads some aspect of your gathering's creative worship.

Eventually, you'll want a leader for each of these teams:

Sacred Space Team: This team plans what the space will look like to enhance the entire worship experience. They may design and set up special interactive prayer stations that correspond with that weekend's theme and teaching. They may set up water basins, clay tables, or other scripturally-based stations for people to worship God through creative expression. They may design certain entry experiences or have props and symbols in the hallways before people come in. They may create and build artistic props that are symbols on which people can write prayers. They might reconfigure the layout of the room for a particular night. They decorate the entry tables and set up candles and anything else used to create a space for worship.

Artists Team: This team may paint artwork to display on the walls for a teaching series. (Usually a teaching series in our gathering runs three to six weeks and the art remains up the whole time.) They may paint creative backdrops for the stages. They may set up paint stations for people to come and paint or draw or write out prayers during a worship gathering. The artists team may have someone share an actual painting and talk about its meaning during the worship gathering. The artists team usually works closely with the Sacred Space team.

Music Team: This team selects the songs to sing at each gathering. This team includes the band members and individuals who select what music is played as people enter and leave the sacred space. They plan any special songs, musical interludes during prayer, etc.

Prayer Team: This team may search for ancient prayers or creeds to be read in the gathering. This team may creatively think of new prayer stations to use. The prayer team leader is an important member of this team, of course. He or she mobilizes prayer for what we do and has a prominent role in planning the worship gatherings.

Digital Arts Team: This team designs and selects the PowerPoint® slides, screen backgrounds, and other digital arts that need to be designed for music lyrics, prayers, creeds, Scripture, etc. In our gathering, a volunteer works with the worship leader to prepare all of the digital artwork each week.

Poetry, Dance, Drama, Video Team(s): The team(s) bring together those who have artistic gifts to contribute to the worship gathering. Some may write prayers or poetry to be read in the gatherings. Some may have a passion to incorporate dance, drama, or the usage of videos in some way. Video jockeys may be commonplace in worship gatherings in the future. They would be responsible for looping and showing images on screens as part of the worship gathering.

Tech Team: There is a lot involved in tech, sound, and lighting, so someone needs to oversee it. In a sense, a tech team is the nervous system of multisensory worship. They can allow a worship gathering to flow technically. This team's leader should always be included in planning meetings.

Teaching Team: The members of this team give the messages in the worship gathering. They should be in the main meetings of this group, so they are part of the whole and not in isolation.

There are many other ways for people in your church community to get involved in the planning of a worship gathering. The key is creating a community-designed gathering. The modern church's very linear worship gatherings were often driven by a solo pastor. But in the emerging church, we are moving from black-and-white approach to a full-color approach.

Solo Pastor Planning   Creative Community Planning

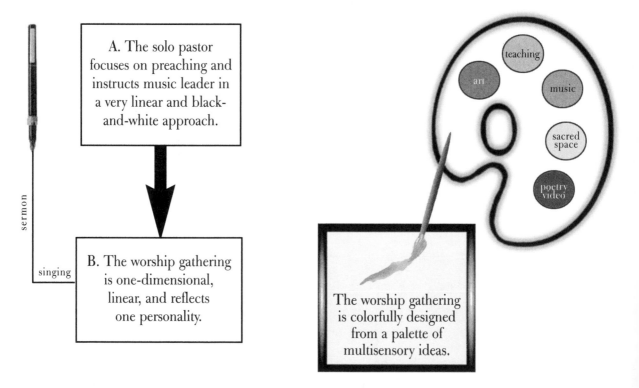

A. The solo pastor focuses on preaching and instructs music leader in a very linear and black-and-white approach.

sermon

singing

B. The worship gathering is one-dimensional, linear, and reflects one personality.

teaching

art

music

sacred space

poetry video

The worship gathering is colorfully designed from a palette of multisensory ideas.

Solo Pastor Planning: The diagram on the left shows how things work when the pastor makes all the decisions (sometimes with the help of a worship leader) and then asks a team of volunteers to implement the plan. This can work well, but it is a highly controlled creative process and will reflect the limited ideas and personality of the pastor. It also limits the creative expression of those in your church, since only one or two individuals are thinking up new ideas.

Creative Community Planning: The second diagram shows a team that meets to come up with ideas together. They are represented by a full palette of creative expressions of worship. They meet well in advance to plan and design the gatherings and assign responsibilities. Each leader builds his or her team. The pastor becomes part of the team rather than giving the team assignments. This group prays together and designs the gathering much as an artist paints a canvas with many colors. For this team, the colors of worship are expressed through a community rather than through a single person.

This team may begin by sketching out an order to the worship gathering, much as one would paint a canvas. I recommend using a whiteboard or sheet of paper to write out an order of the worship gathering (like the samples you will find at the end of each chapter in Part 2). Discuss that order together, add different things, and shape the worship gathering in your community.

You can begin with the theme or Scriptures and then sketch out a design for a worship gathering with different people contributing as you "paint" it together. The music team can suggest and select songs of worship that fit the theme and whatever else may be happening. Your artists may have ideas for paintings to be done and hung around the room for the series. Your digital artists may get an assignment to find artwork online that depicts what you are teaching. Ideas for prayer stations may sprout up from your sacred space team member.

Of course there needs to be a leader who does direct this group and makes the final decisions and wrap up things, but it can be a community worship planning experience.

Depending on the complexity of the worship gathering, detailed notes may need to

"Worship is not an external activity precipitated by the right environment. To worship in spirit is to draw near to God with an undivided heart. We must come in full agreement without hiding anything or disregarding His will."
—Erwin Lutzer

be typed out so the entire leadership knows what is happening. Working together in unison allows for greater creativity and more meaningful times of worship.

We should always recognize that God may want something different! Those involved in a worship gathering should be sensitive to the Holy Spirit's leading and should be prepared to change things when the gathering takes place.

Never Push Jesus to the Sidelines in Designing Worship Gatherings

In our church's creative team, which meets every two weeks to plan and design worship gatherings, we each have a folder containing notes, plans, and the latest ideas. The person that made the folders put a sticker dead center on the cover. The sticker says:

> *May we never allow the creative design of worship*
> *gatherings to push Jesus to the sidelines.*

There is a good reason for this sticker! It reminds our team that we do not simply design programs. We design worship gatherings that are all about Jesus.

It is so easy to get caught up in the cool things churches can do creatively. We can get so caught up in the excitement and fun of creative new ideas that we lose focus of who we do this for and who it is all about.

Someday, when we meet Jesus face to face, it is not going to be about how creative we were or what multisensory things we did in our worship gatherings. We are going to have to give an account of how our hearts worshiped the Lord in the midst of all we did. We'll discover whether we came together for worship in spirit and in truth.

That is why it is so important for those in leadership to pray constantly and to open the Scriptures to make sure they teach God's story and the meaning of being a disciple of Jesus Christ. We should approach designing worship gatherings with trembling, yet excited, hearts.

Emerging worship gatherings change over time. But no matter when or where worship happens, it is all about us laying everything we have down before the throne and saying:

"Holy, Holy, Holy is the Lord God Almighty, who was, and is, and is to come…. You are worthy, our Lord and God, to receive glory and honor and power, for you have created all things, and by your will they were created and have their being" (Revelation 4: 8, 11).

I recommend that you read Revelation 4:8-11 each time your team meets together. We must always keep this image in our minds and hearts as we design worship gatherings.

Taking Care of Your Leaders

We must also watch over those who serve on our worship teams. Planning worship gatherings is a high-intensity ministry. The irony is that it's very easy to burn out those who are leading others in worship. We need to guard against becoming so busy planning worship that we cause them to lose their "first love" (Revelation 2:4) — the One we worship! Beware you don't misuse or fail to shepherd your team.

Emerging Thoughts

1. In your particular church context, how do you envision implementing emerging worship values? Will you do something monthly, weekly, or just make changes in what you currently do?

2. Who currently plans for emerging worship gatherings? Is it a solo approach or a team approach?

3. Which creative worship teams does your church already have in place? Which individuals in your church could form new teams?

4. Have you ever fallen into the trap of pushing Jesus to the side when designing your worship gatherings? How can you prevent that in the future?

5. What do you do to ensure that your worship team members are spiritually healthy and not losing their "first love"?

CHAPTER 9

Approaches Churches Use to Start New Worship Gatherings

We must flatly say that one of the greatest contemporary barriers to meaningful spiritual formation in Christlikeness is the overconfidence in the spiritual efficacy of "regular church services," of whatever kind they may be. Though they are vital, they are not enough. It is that simple.
— Dallas Willard,
Renovation of the Heart

The second half of this book looks at specific ways several churches have started new worship gatherings for emerging generations. I need to say up front that you will read some things in the next couple of chapters that I personally disagree with. You will read how some of the different churches I write about in the next several chapters are even sometimes philosophically opposed to one another. But that is why I am including them!

Agreeing to Disagree about Starting New Worship Gatherings

A wonderful thing about every church's efforts in these next several chapters is that they are at least doing something! They are taking the risk to start something new in their church for emerging generations. Their stories can be a source of inspiration to all of us, no matter which approaches they use.

I respect the leaders in these churches. They aren't sitting around hoping things will magically get better. They aren't waiting around for emerging generations to become part of their existing church. I respect their attitude toward emerging generations — that they are worth the time and effort of trying new things. I respect their willingness to experiment and try new things. I respect their rethinking of what "church" means.

My hope is that their stories will help you move forward in your own journey.

Moving Beyond Deconstruction, Talking, and Thinking

We have talked a lot about postmodernism and about what it means to be the church in emerging culture. However, there comes a time when we need to do something!

The past few years, the emerging church has done a good job of deconstructing things. However, we can't stop there. In the book of Acts, the Athenians and the foreigners "spent their time doing nothing but talking about and listening to the latest ideas" (Acts 17:21). As Christians leaders, we can keep asking "why"? and talking about ideas, but sooner or later we must attempt to do something! We need to experiment and move beyond only rethinking church and worship gatherings. Not only that, we must actually start new ministries, make changes in our churches, and start new worship gatherings or start new churches.

That is what the churches profiled here in Part 2 have done. Most of these churches no longer think of the "church" as the worship gathering. They no longer assume that the church revolves around a single pastor or that everyone must attend the same worship service. When you move past these things, the doors open to innovative thinking. It opens up options for how the local church can structure its new beginning. Let's look at this a little further.

The Traditional Way of Viewing Church

Traditionally a "church" has been primarily defined by a main pastor who leads the whole church (that is, everyone who attends a common worship service). Everyone sits in the sanctuary for the worship service except for maybe youth or children.

In addition to the main worship gathering, the church is supplemented by life-stage groups for teenagers, seniors, parents, small groups, classes, etc. But without a doubt, the church is the worship service. The common defining factor for a church is the worship gathering. This is what is held onto as a "family" and as the "church body."

Traditional Way of Viewing Church

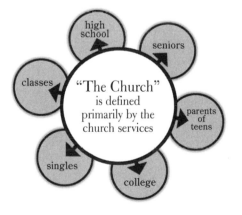

A couple of things shifted this definition of church. For one, this model has an unspoken goal of everyone "sitting in church together." When a church grows, it usually adds a second worship service. So, now there are two meetings. This means the church doesn't all sit together in the same room anymore. That has big ramifications. A church now has people who don't see each other in a worship gathering, yet they are still part of the same "church."

This view of church can be maintained if the same pastor preaches at two or three identical services. There is safety, control, and commonality linked to the senior pastor and the sermon. But what if the senior pastor and the sermon aren't the common link to make a "church" a church?

When we take a theological look at the church, we recognize it is the people united by the Holy Spirit. The meeting, building, and senior pastor don't link it together. This opens up a lot of possibilities.

If we shift our thinking away from the "church" as everyone sitting in the same room for the same worship service under one common pastor and one common teaching, things begin to open up. This is what we discover in the following chapters.

Focus on the Community, not the Worship Service or Pastor

"True worship of God must be a constant and consistent attitude or state of mind within the believer."
—A. W. Tozer

The Bible teaches that the church is a body (1 Corinthians 12) with a plurality of elders overseeing it in a local setting (Acts 14:23, Titus 1:5, 1 Timothy 3). The local church is the intergenerational body life of disciples. We worship God and serve one another on our mission together.

I recently visited a church in San Francisco with four different worship gatherings. They have two English-speaking worship gatherings that are interracial.

Because the church facility is in a very heavily populated Hispanic area, they also have a Hispanic worship service (with a Hispanic pastor leading it).

In addition, they have a Filipino worship gathering due to the large immigrant population in their neighborhood. This meeting is spoken in the language of the people.

This is an exciting thing! This church was able to see itself as more than the worship gathering. They allow a diversity of worship gatherings to happen, each with different leaders — and still see themselves as one church!

An interesting thing is that the Hispanic and Filipino services are accepted without much question. This is a great thing for a church to do. It is a way for different people to be a part of the same church. Everyone worships God in a way the "main church" understands.

Most people wouldn't dream of forcing those in the Hispanic or Filipino worship gatherings to always attend the English worship gatherings in the church. Yet when we propose doing the same exact thing for emerging generations, why is there resistance? They don't realize that, just as with the Hispanics or Filipinos, the differences are cultural.

We are looking at far more than a generational gap. Starting a new worship gathering in a church is missional. It means reaching those of another culture. If we think like this, we can be creative in how we design and rethink our churches!

Looking at Church as a Body (Not a Meeting)

Worship gatherings designed for different people, groups, and mindsets

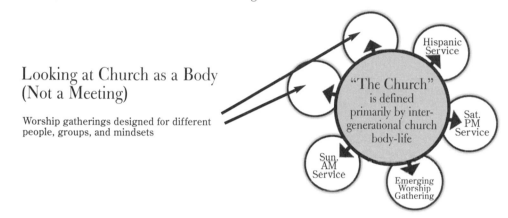

In this second diagram, we see the church defined by intergenerational body life. This can happen in small groups, home groups, home churches, mission trips, and classes. All of these are one body on a mission together. They worship in different gatherings because of different values and approaches to worship.

Looking at it this way, people are the church in their body life throughout the week. That is supplemented with worship gatherings. It is quite opposite from the traditional view!

This diagram shows that the church is one church no matter how many worship gatherings it starts. Perhaps it adds a worship gathering for the local Hispanic population due to language and cultural differences. It may add a more upbeat contemporary Saturday night service. It may then add an emerging worship gathering. Each of these can have different leaders, different sermons, and different

"In my vision at night I looked, and there before me was one like a son of man, coming with the clouds of heaven. He approached the Ancient of Days and was led into his presence. He was given authority, glory and sovereign power; all peoples, nations and men of every language worshiped him."
—Daniel 7:13-14

practices. It doesn't matter! Each service is geared for different population groups with different cultural values.

In many ways, a church can have diverse worship gatherings and still be one church and family. That is, provided the church is not defined by its worship services!

Sadly, this tweaks many church leaders. Our thinking about "church" is ingrained.

Won't This Break Up the Community?

When churches explore this new view of church, many leaders ask, "Won't this break up our community?"

The fact is community does not happen in a worship service unless it is very small and there is a good atmosphere for getting to know one another. If you have more than one worship gathering, you already have a community separation, even if they hear the same sermon.

In most cases, community happens outside of the worship gathering. Community is built up when mentoring happens, when small groups meet, when classes with interaction and dialogue take place, and when people serve together.

Won't this Break Up the Generations?

Many leaders also ask me, "If we start different worship services in our church, won't it break up the generations?" No, not if your church doesn't revolve around the weekend gatherings.

I have yet to see generations connect by simply sitting in a worship gathering at the same time for an hour and a half. We do that when we go to a movie and that doesn't create community. What does connect generations are things that happen outside of the worship gathering — praying together, meeting in the same home churches, serving together, and forming mentoring relationships.

One large church thrived for several decades. The congregation grew older and

"For as I walked around and looked carefully at your objects of worship, I even found an altar with this inscription: TO AN UNKNOWN GOD. Now what you worship as something unknown I am going to proclaim to you."
—Acts 17:23

older and the pastor aged with them. The second generation then got to the point of having children themselves. A whole slice of the church was in their fifties and sixties. Another huge slice was in their twenties and thirties.

The church used the same approaches and methods they had begun with. The older people loved it, but the younger generations grew more and more restless. Eventually, another church in town brought in a younger pastor who related well to the younger generations. A high percentage of younger people left to go to the second church. The first church was left with a gaping hole. This resulted from not thinking ahead or listening to the requests of the younger generations.

Many of the churches discussed in the second half of this book avoided this tragedy by thinking ahead. By starting new worship gatherings and ministries, they have allowed their worship community to diversify and prevented unnecessary losses.

How Will People Know the Senior Pastor?

Usually senior pastors alone ask me, "But how will people know who I am?" I usually reply by asking three critical questions: Why does everyone need to know who a church's senior pastor is? Why do the people have to see one person as the leader? After all, Jesus is the head of the church, isn't he?

This is so important I've written a heartfelt letter about it.

ADDITIONAL CHAPTERS ONLINE
FOR SENIOR PASTORS

Visit www.vintagefaith.com to read a very important chapter:
A Personal Plea to Senior Pastors. This Web chapter supplements
many of the things spoken about senior pastors here.

Interestingly, some churches have tried starting experimental worship gatherings.

They add some candles around the room, use different music, and then show a videotape of the senior pastor's teaching. This solves the concern of making the senior pastor known! I will be the first to agree that God uses all types of churches and methods. God even uses churches that play a video of the pastor in their "emerging worship" gatherings. Lots of people attend these video gatherings. This approach is not explored in this book, however, since it goes against most emerging worship values.

I recently talked to someone in her twenties who was visiting a church where they did this, and she explained how to her there was an incredible clash of values in a worship gathering like this. She also explained how bizarre it was to her seeing a screen drop, and then someone who obviously was from an entirely different culture begin a message that was entirely geared for a different mindset.

Again, I know God works in many ways, and there are video churches who are very successful with emerging generations. But I wouldn't rush into that for a post-Christian culture. Be very careful of what you do. Please rethink what this communicates to generations who are already skeptical of the church. Rethink what this looks like to generations who are seeking spiritual gurus, mystics, prophets, and instead after a time of perhaps meditative, reflective music, prayer, candles, etc., suddenly a big-screen TV preacher drops down in the midst of an environment that is much different than the one who now is preaching.

The values emerging among post-Christians are to decentralize leadership and personalities in a church, rather than propagate them — especially by video! I believe older pastors should be training and mentoring younger pastors to be the preachers and leaders of these new worship gatherings, rather than be trained to be the sub-pastor who sets up the time for the video to come on before someone else preaches. To a modern mindset the video concept works great; it's perfectly aligned! So I know these can be successful! And there are a lot of modern-minded younger people who were born into a Judeo-Christian worldview. So there may be lots of modern-minded younger people with whom this works great! But don't assume this will work as easily with post-Christian generations.

Rethinking "Youth" and "Young Adult" Ministry Categories

Many churches gear and promote emerging worship gatherings to "young adults." I'd like to examine this phrase and life-stage briefly.

If you do a search on the Web to see how "young adult" is used, you'll discover the only groups using this phrase to refer to people between eighteen to 35 years of age are churches. Almost everyone else in our culture uses the phrase to refer to teenagers! The Young Adult Library Association, for instance, categorizes young adults as those between the ages of 12 and 18.

Why has the church adopted the phrase "young adults" to speak about people up to 35 or even 40 years of age? We started "college" ministries to cater to those pursuing post-secondary education. Then we created ministries for twentysomethings. Then with people remaining single into midlife, we create a larger "young adult" category. We kept adding years to a ministry category that can inadvertently hinder people from moving into real adult life-stages.

In biblical times, when someone reached the age of 13, he or she was considered an adult and fully incorporated into the religious community.

We live in a different cultural setting. Yet, we can still profit from rethinking youth ministry in the midst of change in the church. Our goal should be to see youth holistically brought into church life. Many youth want to become part of emerging worship gatherings, which is why the issue is so pressing.

The "youth" category in our churches needs to be rethought. More time should be spent recognizing that teenagers are young adults and preparing them for adulthood. The reality is that teenagers face adult situations regularly. It is a disservice to say they aren't "young adults" until they're eighteen years old.

I recently heard of one church that encourages 40-year-olds to be part of their "young adult" ministry. It is more than a little weird to call someone who is old enough to be a parent a "young adult." At age 40, you could be a grandparent! No wonder many people in the "young adult" age range aren't maturing spiritually. We've provided a glorified youth ministry for them. Instead, these adults should be fully integrated into the life of the church.

The more I ponder the whole idea of "youth" and "young adult" categories, the more uncomfortable I feel. We have lost intergenerational relationships in church by keeping everyone segmented into programmatic departments. I am all for developing ministries for life-stages. The church can help people deal with common issues of life. But it is not healthy in the long-term to create "young adult" worship gatherings.

That is one reason why Graceland moved from being a "young adult" worship gathering to an all-age worship gathering. This allowed us to focus on building a distinct college ministry without restricting certain age groups from the main gathering. Emerging worship gatherings are not for people within a certain age range.

Ways Churches Start New Gatherings and New Churches

In the next section, we will look at ways a handful of churches have started new worship gatherings for emerging generations.

At Santa Cruz Bible Church, we went through virtually every approach covered in this book. We started Graceland as a life-stage worship gathering within the church. Then we went to an all-age worship gathering and community that existed almost entirely independently within the church. We next shifted to keeping the worship gathering going but folding all the leadership teams into one larger all-church team. This eventually morphed into a new church, Vintage Faith Church.

Vintage Faith Church is a sister-hybrid-church of Santa Cruz Bible Church. We are independent but share things too! You'll hear our personal story and the reasons for what we now do in chapter 13.

As you read through these next chapters, please remember that every church is still in process. They are experimenting and pioneering things. None is an ideal model of how to do things. I hope their examples will stir your thinking about what you want to do (or not do) with your church.

The following chapters are structured in this way:

- Why a new worship gathering was needed in a particular church
- How the new worship gathering functions within the whole church
- How the leadership is structured in the whole church
- What the new emerging worship gathering looks like
- Summary and closing thoughts

Emerging Thoughts

1. Have you ever thought about how "church" typically revolves around people attending a common worship service to hear the same sermon with the same pastor?

2. Do you agree or disagree with the second diagram that shows church as "people" with the larger worship gatherings placed outside the center?

3. Have you experienced any of the concerns about starting a new worship gathering listed in this chapter? Have you experienced any other concerns?

CHAPTER 10

Starting a Life-Stage Outreach Gathering

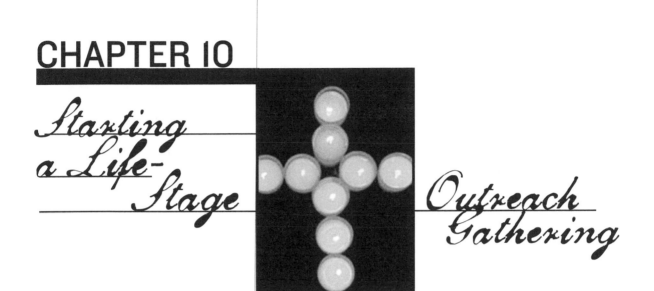

The greatest thing I respect about Willow Creek Community Church is their passion about seeing non-Christians come to know Jesus. It is in their blood and in their history. One cannot attend a Willow Creek convention or listen to Bill Hybels speak without being stirred and motivated to have an evangelistic heart. Another thing I respect about Willow Creek is their willingness to experiment and try new things.

In 1996, Willow Creek experimented by starting a seeker service called "Axis" designed to reach young adults. Let's take a look at Willow Creek's experiment with a worship service and ministry specifically designed to reach and disciple emerging generations.

1. Why a new worship gathering was needed

An Inside Look at Willow Creek Community Church describes their reasons behind starting a new worship gathering for emerging generations:

"Churches around the world of every size, denomination and socioeconomic background are experiencing a similar phenomenon: They look at their pews and see a solid representation of middle-aged families all the way through to the elderly. Their junior and senior high youth groups are still surviving. But look for someone in the 18-30-something age range, and you are left with a desolate feeling; there is a generation missing."

Willow Creek has been used by God in tremendous ways to reach thousands upon thousands of people in their local community. This is due in part to their design of a weekend seeker-service. It gives people in the church a place to bring their non-believing friends.

Despite the incredibly amazing success God gave them, though, by the 1990s they were missing a generation or two. In retrospect, they realized that what happened was not isolated to Willow Creek. A cultural shift was occurring. Growing up in a post-Christian culture means that emerging generations had philosophical and spiritual beliefs and values that were different from previous generations. The way Willow Creek had historically designed their weekend seeker-service was not effective at engaging emerging generations. Willow Creek realized they needed to do something and their Axis ministry was born.

Birthing a New Seeker Service for "18-20-Somethings"

In 1996, the Axis seeker-service and ministry began. Axis is promoted and designed for "18-20-somethings." The first Axis service started on Saturday nights so they could share the children's ministry with the main seeker-services at Willow Creek. They also added a Sunday morning Axis service at 11:15.

Axis has various communities developed within the ministry to connect and shepherd people. They have a college-age ministry, a ministry for young couples, and a group for singles in the post-college twenty-something age range.

Axis strongly focuses on social justice. They do construction with Habitat for Humanity, serve the homeless, work with inner city children, and meet with teenagers in a local juvenile center. The Axis community does a lot throughout the week in addition to their weekend services.

A major part of their overall strategy goes beyond Axis itself and ties it into the whole church community at Willow Creek.

2. How the worship gathering functions within the whole church

Because Axis is considered an outreach service to the "18-20-somethings," their goal is move people into attending the all-church midweek worship service geared for believers of all ages. Willow Creek calls this their "New Community" that meets on Wednesday and Thursday nights. Those in Axis experience deeper teaching at the intergenerational New Community gatherings. They also take communion together.

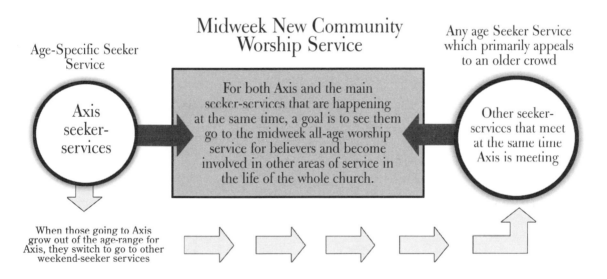

Nancy Ortberg was the primary Axis leader for several years (before recently moving to Menlo Park, California, with her husband, John Ortberg). She explained to me: "Axis is a pipeline into the main church. Axis serves as a ministry where people in their twenties go. As they get married and have children, they are encouraged to shift over to the other weekend services of the church."

She mentioned how they coach their small group leaders to help people make the transition over to the midweek New Community service for believers and then to the other weekend services when they get older.

Since Axis is specifically an "18-20-something" service, it is neither a church nor a separate community. It is a life-stage community within a whole church, like a high school ministry would function in most churches. Axis is more or less an entry point or "pipeline" into the whole church.

Although the other weekend services are open for any age, they mainly cater to those who are 30 and older. Axis isn't strict about asking people to leave when they hit 30 years of age. They do encourage them to be involved in leadership, however, if they still want to be part of Axis.

3. How leadership is structured in the whole church

Nancy Ortberg explains: "The Axis staff has very minimal interaction with the other staff of Willow Creek. One of the great gifts we have is that we have been given a very long leash. We aren't controlled or told what to do. I personally report to someone on the Willow Creek Management Team who keeps a pulse on what happens with Axis. I don't report directly to Bill Hybels. I then lead the Axis staff and report to the Management Team about Axis. In terms of elders, we don't have specific elders who are part of Axis or elders who go to Axis. But we do have their involvement when needed, usually for problems and when we need help."

Although Bill Hybels is the senior pastor of Willow Creek, he rarely ever goes to or speaks at Axis. Not everyone in Axis even knows who Bill Hybels is, unless they go to the other weekend services where he normally speaks. But Bill does keep abreast of what is happening in Axis through the Management Team.

According to Nancy, "A sign of unity in a church is not if they know the senior pastor, but if they have the same DNA. It isn't about a person; it is about Jesus Christ."

Nancy adds: "The Axis staff meets on its own. However, we do have a once a month meeting where the small group staff of all the departments of the church (including the Axis small group staff) come together for training. Small groups are a major emphasis for Willow

Creek, so this keeps small groups at the forefront.

"We also have an all-Willow Creek staff meeting every few months where all the staff of Willow Creek comes together for general information, but apart from that we keep pretty distinct."

Axis builds its own leadership teams and functions very much on its own in terms of actual ministry, including their own retreats. But they make sure to have "touch points" with the rest of Willow Creek so they don't lose touch with the whole church and its vision.

A critical touch point is having the same DNA as the rest of Willow Creek. Willow Creek's DNA is its core values and "Five G's." The Five G's are marking points for members and are used to set goals: Grace (salvation), Growth (sanctification), Group (small groups and community), Gifts (serving), and Good Stewardship (honoring God with resources).

Setting their goals by this list keeps Axis aligned with every other ministry at Willow Creek. By focusing their goals, they experience harmony with the whole church. Axis teaches the Five G's through their membership process. Strategically, people don't become members of Axis, per se; they become members of Willow Creek and go through the same membership teaching materials as everyone else in the church.

4. What an Axis worship gathering looks like

Axis is actually a "seeker service" with the goal of moving people into the midweek worship service for believers. This is where the cultural changes among emerging generations begin to take an interesting twist.

Historically at Willow Creek's weekend seeker-service, the goal was to remove as many spiritual symbols and spiritual terminology as possible in order to be seeker-friendly. Apart from one congregational song, historically they don't even have musical singing as part of worship.

The weekend seeker services at Willow Creek primarily attract those who have had some sort of bad experience with the church being dry, dead, and ritualistic. In response to this, the seeker services use joyful music, life, drama, and excellent teaching, and God has used this to save thousands upon thousands of individuals.

With today's culture changes, however, a seeker service for emerging generations has a different set of values.

Emerging generations are not turned off by spiritual terms, by worshipful singing, or by religious symbols. In fact that is exactly what "emerging seekers" are hoping to find if they go to a church gathering. For this reason, Axis has a different design to their meetings than other weekend seeker-services at Willow Creek. They still think through the lingo and the program in terms of what a seeker would experience and think. The Axis service, however, pays attention to different things than other Willow Creek services, including aesthetics.

Paying Attention to Aesthetics

Axis meets in the Willow Creek gymnasium, but plans to move into the main worship center as soon as the new Willow Creek building is completed. They will redesign the entire worship center when they move. While they still meet in the gym, they work hard to change the aesthetics of the room.

Brown heavy curtains are hung at angles to help with the sound and create a certain look and feel. They are striving for a "raw" look in Axis in contrast to the more polished aesthetics of the other services at Willow Creek. They set up a stage with drapery, fabric, and other structures built behind it. They set up a coffee bar in the rear of the room with couches set up for people to hang out, like a living room.

Initially, they tried using tables in the room so there wouldn't be rows of chairs. They found that tables were not ideal, though, because people didn't want to face one another during the service. So they moved to rows of chairs facing the stage instead. Each service allows people to leave their chairs to do something experiential and interactive.

Multisensory Worship in the Design of Axis

Each week is different at the Axis gatherings. They don't use the same worship elements every week. But they do use a multisensory approach to worship in their gatherings.

Once they took sheets and draped them all around the front of the room at various angles. They then ran video projectors showing the Jesus film on the sheets. When people walked into the room, they saw images of Jesus at different angles. This kept going throughout the whole service. It enhanced their focus on Jesus beyond what was said in the message.

The Axis service usually starts with a performance song that ties into the theme of the service and is also one that people would recognize from the radio. Because Axis is considered a "seeker service," constant attention is given to what is happening in the culture of "18-20-somethings." This is used to build bridges of identification to them. They might have a video clip from a popular movie or drama related to that weekend's theme.

A unique interactive element in Axis gatherings is asking a question and then giving people a few minutes to discuss it among themselves. This raises the value of community. One woman in her twenties who visited Axis told me this interactive question was her favorite part of the Axis service. What she liked about it was that it wasn't the usual "Say hello to your neighbor and tell them that God loves them" sort of a thing that many churches do in a greeting time. There was a specific question asked that tied into the Axis teaching theme of the service and got her thinking and involved. It also introduced her to two or three other people sitting around her with whom she ended up having more conversation after the service ended.

Teaching and Musical Worship Response

The typical Axis message is approximately 30 minutes long. Often the messages are topical and directly tie into the issues of life that someone in the "18-20-something" age range deals with or is interested in. They use teaching series such as "Axis @ The Movies," "Jesus 3-D," "Love, Lust, and Loneliness," and "Starbuck's Spirituality."

After the message, they have a time of musical worship that sets the Axis seeker-services apart from the other weekend services at Willow Creek. Axis believes that musical worship is correctly placed after a teaching message, because it is a natural response to what it taught.

"When this age is over, and the countless millions of the redeemed fall on their faces before the throne of God, missions will be no more. It is a temporary necessity. But worship abides forever."
—John Piper

Axis believes worship is not just singing. They incorporate worshipful responses using both singing and other interactive and participatory approaches. They encourage people to leave their seats during the singing and respond in different ways. They use prayer stations. They have had stations where people watch images on TV screens and write responses on paper or cards. They have had a wall of names where you could kneel down and pray for people.

After a message on relationships, they set up stations where people were encouraged to write letters to other people they had hurt in order to ask for forgiveness. One service focused on helping the poor. As an application, they had people take off their shoes and donate them to the poor right there. They walked out of that service without their shoes!

Axis tries to teach that worship means sacrifice and response. That is why they design some sort of response after each teaching message. They also take an offering each week. An Axis Service lasts about 60 to 70 minutes.

4. Summary and closing thoughts

It is fascinating and encouraging to know that Axis and Willow Creek, the premier seeker-church of America, is so successful, but still doesn't feel they have it all figured out. I admire their experimentation and willingness to allow new forms of emerging worship to develop within Axis. It takes humility from the Willow Creek staff to admit that what they do in their main weekend services does not necessarily resonate with emerging generations.

It takes security on the part of Bill Hybels to not be in the midst of Axis, trying to control or shape it. Axis is given freedom, which probably explains why it is able to thrive and grow as it does.

From talking with Nancy Ortberg, I also admire that they are recognizing that emerging generations have different values. What's next? Nancy explained: "My dream and vision is that there would be regional expressions of Axis, but I don't think video would work. I think for the generation I work with, some sort of regional expression would have to be more like a church plant with live people teaching, not a video." This would allow the development of more emerging teachers and preachers. I personally agree with this, as many of the values of emerging generations (especially unchurched) go against the idea of a video-preacher. I respect that Axis and Willow Creek are training and empowering younger communicators and preachers instead of reproducing by video sermons.

Generational Preferences or a Cultural Mindset Shift?

My primary questions about the approach Axis and Willow Creek use are: What is the longer term outlook on the "experiment" of starting a life-stage worship service for young adults? Is emerging worship something for a specific age group or is it truly for a different cultural mindset? I ask these questions because cultural mindsets transcend age. The postmodern cultural shift definitely reaches beyond a certain age group.

If we are talking about a mindset, then to make someone switch to another approach of spiritual formation and worship when they hit a certain age is a difficult undertaking. It would be like birthing a Korean worship service that uses Korean language, Korean music, and a Korean mindset in all of their communications and then — when the people hit a certain age — telling them they can't worship as Koreans anymore.

Similarly, it has to be difficult for someone who resonates with experiential multisensory worship and is used to interactive worship to turn a certain age and suddenly be told they have to attend the "main" services. Was their worship in the other gathering invalid? Virtually every church I know of that's tried this finds the forced transition invalid.

On the other hand, if we look at a life-stage worship gathering in a modern thinking church which targets primarily younger and more modern thinking people like the rest of the church, it may make sense to do it this way. It is like the high school ministry that caters to the teenagers in church who grew up with a Judeo-Christian worldview. It depends on who the church is reaching and what the church is doing with its worship gathering and ministry.

If Axis removed its "18-20-something" label, I wonder if a lot of people from all ages would resonate with what they do? Plenty of people over the age of 30 would thrive in and connect to the worship culture Axis has established. But then this would make it a "worship service" and change its whole strategy in Willow Creek. Still a worthy experiment, in my opinion.

Is Axis a Seeker Service or Worship Gathering?

Another interesting question: Since Axis as a seeker service has been responding to the cultural changes and recognizing that "emerging seekers" want to be in a place of worship, how does this change things? Axis now includes a lot of worship in different forms. They use about four songs in worship now. For those wanting more "singing," there's the midweek New Community believer's service. However, for a lot of people the "singing" part at Axis is sufficient for one's worship response.

How you define "worship" is important, because at Axis they always have worship that is more than singing through the prayer stations and other things that occur after the message.

The teaching at New Community is definitely geared for believers, where at Axis they make sure the teaching is understood by both non-believers and believers. This is a difference. Again, the whole philosophy of preaching and teaching needs to be taken into consideration. Is the worship service the place people should look to for their weekly "feeding"? Or does that happen throughout the week? And is preaching in a one-way format the way emerging generations learn best? Is attending two worship services a week the best thing for one's spiritual formation in terms of how time is spent?

The strategy of going to Axis (which seems very much like a worship service) and then coming back for another worship service (with some more singing and teaching geared for believers) is an interesting issue to think about.

Apart from having different generations all sitting in the same room for an hour or so, why come back again midweek if Axis already provides worship and teaching? Shouldn't the generations mix in other ways outside of simply sitting in a big meeting together? Relational community happens best in small groups—the third G tells us that!

Common vision and information is passed on at New Community. But community is about more than common vision and information. At the time of writing this book, only half of the Axis community goes to the midweek New Community service. That tells me something.

People have limited time. A second large group worship gathering seems redundant when people could use that time to join a small group, help others, or to be light and witnesses for the Kingdom outside the walls of the church building. It all depends on how one views the Axis service (as a worship gathering or seeker service). To me, Axis sounds like a worship gathering where believers worship and non-believers see God at work.

I imagine that as Willow Creek adapts, transitions, and reads the cultural signs of the times, Axis will do the same. I'm sure we will see them continue to learn, explore what works, and find better ways to make disciples.

It is thrilling to know that a church like Willow Creek is open to experimenting. They are adapting and changing along with the culture. Emerging worship happens at Axis.

I look forward to seeing what God does next with their "experiment"!

Sample Worship Gathering

Axis at Willow Creek Community Church

Series Title
Love Life: God Loving You

Gathering Goal/Focus
For people to feel that God loves them and grasp the wonder of his love, not just be told about it.

On Screens as People Walk In

Scrolling Scriptures selected from 1 John (*The Message* paraphrase) tie into that evening's theme. The Scripture passages are broken up into different key phrases and artistically shown on the screens.

Prelude Song

Band plays to signal that the gathering is now beginning. High energy music gets people in the door, in their seats, and ready.

Worship Song

"He Reigns" gets people out of their seats, engages them in the wonder of God, and unifies the room in worship.

Welcome

After people are greeted, a question is raised. People are given time to talk with one another about possible answers.

Offering and Announcements

People are told: "This is the time in our service when we receive the offering. This time is for those of us who call God our Father and Axis our home. If you are new to Axis, or are still figuring out faith, please don't feel any pressure to give." Bags are passed while announcements are made.

Poetry Reading

The poem "The In Between of Days" is read live on stage, with black and white images shown on the screens to accompany the poem. The images narrate the story of a woman waiting by a window in her house, drinking a cup of coffee and wondering internally about life and faith.

Message

The teaching pastor uses many images on the screens, including pictures and text graphics. He frequently uses props to illustrate his points. He also uses a flip chart.

Song and Response

A woman sings "Amazing Grace" a capella. This song is sung from an extended thrust stage that goes sixteen feet into the audience so she can stand in the middle of the room. People can sit, meditate, and dwell in "grace" as the song reinforces the theme of how much God loves us.

Worship and Prayer

During a time of musical worship, the Axis staff stands along the thrust stage on both sides. Anyone who has trouble "feeling" God's love, or who wonders if God could love them, is asked to walk forward to talk and pray with a staff member. People continue to walk up and pray with the staff while the worship songs "Hallelujah, Your Love Is Amazing," "Amazing Love," and "Forever" are sung. Visuals appear on the side and center screens all throughout this time.

Closing

The worship gathering ends with a "Letter from God." It is a passage from Henri Nouwen's book *Life of the Beloved,* which incorporates several passages about God's love from the Psalms into the form of a letter. It serves as a closing benediction.

CHAPTER 11

Creating Life-Stage Worship Gatherings

What is probably the most common way churches have used to start new emerging worship gatherings? Typically, a church notices it is getting older and missing a generation or two in its midst. So begins a new, full-fledged, worship gathering designed for "young adults" ages 18 to 35.

The strategy is that these "young adults" will eventually phase over into the "main" worship gathering in the church as they get older. Instead, almost without exception, something happens after a few years that causes church leaders to rethink a few things again.

The Eventual Struggle of "Young Adult" Worship Gatherings

As the community in an emerging worship gathering ages, its older members don't outgrow their preference for worship style and approach to worship and spiritual formation. When they get to the age they need to leave, it's not something most want to do. People don't change their expression of worship when they turn 35. They desire to worship God in the way they've become accustomed. So moving them into a worship gathering that feels different, looks different, and has different values is not easy to do.

Because of this difficulty, most "young adult" worship gatherings eventually become all-age worship gatherings. This is very freeing and validates the ministry as a full-fledged worship gathering instead of simply a sub-ministry of the church.

Adding Another Emerging Worship Gathering for Younger "Young Adults"

Interestingly, as the new emerging worship gathering ages, it eventually can also lose its appeal among younger people in their late teens and early 20s. This is what happened at McLean Bible Church and the story we will look at in this chapter.

McLean Bible Church was one of the first churches in America to recognize the changes going on in our culture. They experimented by starting an emerging worship gathering and ministry designed for 18- to 35-year-olds called "Frontline."

Years later, McLean Bible Church has lessened the focus on age in their Frontline worship gathering. They've also created a new worship community, "The Gathering," designed for even younger adults. Let's take a look at their story.

1. Why a new worship gathering was needed

McLean Bible Church is a very large and thriving congregation in the suburbs of Washington, D.C. A few years ago, the elders of the church realized that — even though the church was very successful — the 18- to 35-year-old adult population was largely missing in their church. They hired a new staff member, Ken Baugh, to begin a brand-new ministry for these young adults.

McLean was one of the first churches to specifically focus on this age group in a more holistic way. They recognized a desire and need for a different type of worship gathering. When they started Frontline, it was a full-fledged worship gathering considered equal with the other weekend services at the church. This was almost unheard of at the time. Most churches had a "college group" or a sub-ministry for those in their 20s to supplement the main worship gathering. But starting an actual worship gathering specifically for them was something brand new.

2. How the worship gathering functions in the whole church

Ken Baugh was hired to develop a young adult worship gathering and to develop leadership and small groups for McLean Bible Church's new Frontline ministry and community. From the beginning, they knew to focus on holistic spiritual formation in the life of a young adult, and not just the worship gathering. It looked like it was off to a good start, but they soon learned their first lesson.

There was a refreshing burst of energy that came from starting a worship gathering and having music that catered to a young adult population. However, the senior pastor — a very gifted communicator — preached the same message in Frontline as in the other services for consistency's sake. The senior pastor did wear jeans instead of a suit and tie, but the Frontline worship gathering didn't grow the way they had hoped. Then something was discovered by mistake. The senior pastor took a sabbatical for the summer but the church's leadership decided to keep Frontline going while he was away.

Ken and a team of younger adults took this opportunity to change the way the worship gathering was designed. The team thought through more than just the music style. The preaching became more narrative and didn't necessarily reflect the main service's message. They added videos as part of the communication and worship experience. They brought in some interactive approaches to worship with art and visuals. As a result of all these changes, and of letting younger adults lead and preach, Frontline doubled in size during the senior pastor's absence.

This raised an interesting question when the senior pastor came back! What should they do now?

"Come, let us bow down in worship, let us kneel before the LORD our Maker."
—Psalm 95:6

The senior pastor, who is an outstanding preacher and leader, demonstrated great wisdom and humility. He allowed Ken and the Frontline team to continue what they were doing. This made Frontline all the more distinct from what happened in the other services. The senior pastor still comes in a few times a year to speak. The rest of the year, Ken and other Frontline staff preach and oversee everything.

A Focus on Small Groups that Influenced the Whole Church

Because community is so highly valued among emerging generations, high attention was paid to discipleship in small groups from the beginning.

Frontline still has about 80 percent of its community in small groups. That is an exceptionally high percentage, showing that they really take small group seriously.

This passion for small groups and community in turn influenced the rest of the church. The church took Frontline's lead. Eventually the pastor of small groups within Frontline began leading and developing small groups for the entire church.

Loosening the Age Boundaries

Frontline was originally designed to be a life-stage worship gathering and ministry for people ages 18 to 35. When someone moved past that age range, they were supposed to move into the other worship gatherings led by the senior pastor. In a way, the church was comprised of worshiping communities in two distinct age categories.

After time, however, they realized that maintaining an age group demographic for a worship gathering was not working as smoothly as they had planned. Frontline has now stopped enforcing the age parameter. They still call it a "young adult" ministry. They still have age-specific leadership roles, retreats, and other events. But rather than focus all the attention on moving people from one worship gathering to the other, they now focus on seeing the people of Frontline become part of McLean Bible Church at large.

"When the offerings were finished, the king and everyone present with him knelt down and worshiped."
—2 Chronicles 29:29

Their goal is to see people in Frontline serve in other areas of the church such as youth ministry or children's ministry. This is one way individuals in Frontline can give back to McLean Bible Church in appreciation for all they've done to intentionally reach emerging generations.

As Frontline Ages, Another Worship Gathering Starts

Allowing Frontline to age raised another issue.

Frontline initially started for people who at the time were 18 to 35 years old. They catered specifically to the young suburban professionals in and around Washington, D.C.

Over time, it became apparent that the emerging population of new, younger adults did not resonate with the Frontline worship gathering approach.

McLean Bible Church stepped out again. They started a new worship gathering called "The Gathering" that currently caters to younger adults ages 18 to 25. The Gathering is quite different from Frontline in many ways.

Each of the three worship gatherings at McLean Bible Church has its own pastor.

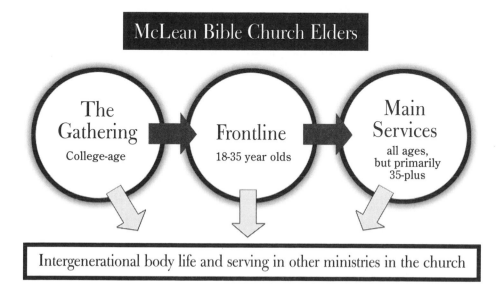

The pastors do not preach the same messages. Each one has age-specific definitions, but they don't hold to them tightly. All three gatherings desire to see those in the worshiping communities become part of the entire church's body life through various things happening outside of the worship services themselves.

3. How the leadership is structured in the whole church

It is unique to have three different worship communities within the same church. The pastor of The Gathering, Denny Henderson, reports to the Frontline pastor, Ken Baugh. Denny is not an elder, but attends all the elder meetings to represent the ministry. He is also on the church's executive team. Ken Baugh reports directly to the senior pastor. His title is associate senior pastor for the whole church. Ken preaches in the main services of McLean Bible Church about seven to ten times a year in order to bridge relationships between the separate services.

It is in the realm of possibility that when the senior pastor retires, Ken could become the senior pastor for the whole church. When considering how difficult is usually is for a church to transition between senior pastors, this may be a good option for other churches to consider.

Each worship gathering has a specific staff team. These teams meet and function independently. Once a month, an all-staff meeting brings together the staff of Frontline and The Gathering with the rest of the church's staff. The Gathering staff also joins the Frontline staff for a special meeting once a month. The different staffs are given as much freedom and autonomy as possible, while maintaining a sense of togetherness.

4a. What a Frontline worship gathering looks like

Frontline meets in the same building as the main worship gatherings do, so their setup options are limited. They add screens to display graphics and other art. They dim the lights and create various tones and colors in the room through lighting. The volume of music is intentionally louder.

The night begins with a worship song. One of the staff members welcomes people. Every week a volunteer Frontline ministry leader is profiled. The leader describes how he or she serves God. This encourages others to serve God and shows that Frontline is not all about the staff. Frontline is a community, so they intentionally place attention on many disciples of Jesus.

A Scripture video plays weekly. That evening's Scripture passage is creatively presented on the screens using art, nature scenes, and Flash animation.

Next is 15 or 20 minutes of worship through song. After the message, a reflective wrap-up song and prayer wrap up the evening's gathering.

When Frontline has communion, the cross becomes the theme and central focus of the gathering. Artists are unleashed to create paintings, sculpture, and other worshipful expressions. This artwork is displayed in a central place where it can be incorporated into that evening's worship experience.

4b. What The Gathering looks like

The Gathering takes things a bit further than Frontline does. Upon entering The Gathering worship service, the lights are even dimmer. They desire to set up a "raw" urban stage and environment. They use dimmed colored lighting, but do not spotlight the band members or singers.

Where Frontline incorporates a lot of video and more upbeat rock-pop music. The Gathering goes low key with video and the music is more traditional, which appeals to younger adults.

The Gathering doesn't use performance songs or solo songs as Frontline does. They incorporate as many songs as possible written by individuals within The Gathering community. Many of these songs are written like traditional hymns, with the lyrics communicating theology.

The Gathering starts off every worship time with a two-minute video that recaps the week before. The video is a mix of images, Scriptures, and thematic graphics or short excerpts of the sermon from the past week. After the video ends, there is a formal call to

"The most valuable thing the Psalms do for me is to express the same delight in God which made David dance."
—C. S. Lewis

worship through the reading of Scripture.

Respect for the Scripture reading is seen in people quickly becoming quiet and taking their seats. After the call to worship, 35 minutes of worship through singing and prayer begins. They often stop to teach the Scriptural meaning behind each song.

Denny Henderson, the pastor of The Gathering, is the primary teacher. He usually uses a narrative approach and teaches through books of the Bible. Before every message, the whole Gathering community says out loud a statement of belief about the Bible. The Gathering chooses to use few projected images to keep the focus on the Scriptures. They actively encourage people to bring their Bibles into the worship gathering and also provide a lot of Bibles for people to read and keep. The message is around forty minutes long, and then more musical worship follows. A prayer ends the evening meeting. Offering is not formally taken, but there are wooden boxes in various places in the room for people to give their offerings.

Like many other emerging worship gatherings, The Gathering tries to get people out of their seats as often as possible in order to interact during the musical worship time. They set up prayer stations with prayer journals. They have had different forms of art stations for people to paint at. One evening, they encouraged a communal painting on a huge canvas.

Another time, The Gathering had an evening of total silence. From the moment people walked in, there was no sound. Instead of the normal call to worship when a person would normally read Scripture from the stage, they put the verses on the screens while the room remained silent. There was no band and no singing. The lyrics to the songs were put on the screens while everyone sat in silence.

When it came time for the sermon, the message was written on the screen for everyone to read. Not a word was spoken. There was simply silence and meditation.

5. Summary and closing thoughts

It's refreshing to see a church like McLean Bible Church that believes in the importance of investing facilities, staff, and finances into emerging generations. It's refreshing to see a senior pastor who recognizes and accepts the changes happening in our culture and who does not see himself as the only person who can preach to and shepherd emerging generations. That is part of the reason Frontline and The Gathering have thrived for as long as they have.

I think it is great that the Frontline pastor attends part of the elder meetings, but I wonder if The Gathering pastor should also be there? I also wonder if it wouldn't be beneficial having elders who are actually part of Frontline and The Gathering there, too. I imagine that if these new worship gatherings are equal with the "main" one, then elders should represent them and know their ongoing issues, joys, and struggles.

Will Life-Stage Worship Gatherings Work in the Long Run?

These worship gatherings started as age-specific worship gatherings and have only recently relaxed their age boundaries. I wonder if Frontline and The Gathering will eventually become all-age worship gatherings to allow all those who resonate with emerging worship to be involved.

They then can focus on building intergenerational relationships and community outside the worship gathering, and people can stay in the worshiping community they resonate with as long as they want. If not, to me, it will be a constant struggle to not become a glorified youth group to some degree.

The leadership of McLean Bible Church freely admits that they constantly adapt, change, and experiment as they go. That is to be commended! Their passion to see emerging generations worship God is very respectable. What is even more respectable is that they are more concerned with spiritual formation and discipleship than with the worship gatherings.

We shall see through time how God leads McLean Bible Church in their experiment, innovation, and passion for ministering to the emerging generations in their area.

"Lawful worship consists in obedience alone."
—John Calvin

Sample Worship Gathering

Frontline at McLean Bible Church

Opening Song
"We Are Hungry"

Welcome & Greeting
An introduction to the night.

Video
Each Frontline worship gathering incorporates Scripture in a creative video on the screens. The Scripture focuses on what Frontline teaches at the gathering.

Worship Set
"Hungry (Falling On My Knees)," "May the Words," "He is the Love," and "O Praise Him (All This for a King)." Graphics and art serve as backdrops to the worship lyrics.

Offering and Song
While the offering is taken, the song "The Eyes of My Heart" is sung. The song sets up the message.

Message
Creativity is used to communicate through various artwork and graphics during the 30- to 40-minute message. Artistic props or other participatory elements may be used.

Closing Song
"Take My Life"

Announcements
Announcements present ways for people to get involved in the Frontline community as easily as possible.

Sample Worship Gathering

The Gathering at McLean Bible Church

Series Title
Unashamed

Sermon Title
Romans: Volume IV

Opening Video
The opening video is a creative compilation of the previous week's sermon and prayers. It has funky music loops, the voices are altered, and the screens display creative imagery that relate to the series and the previous week's sermon.

Call to Worship
The band picks up the music loop from the video and begins to play as someone gives a formal call to worship through prayer and Scripture (Hebrews 10:10-12, 14, 19-23). Everything is designed to flow together without breaks. The goal is to have the night feel like one giant moment (rather than feel fragmented with different elements).

Song One
A newly written song, "Anthem," focuses on Hebrews 10. All songs are transitioned and bridged naturally by computer-generated loops (song one and two bleed into each other, just as song two and three bleed into each other without a break).

Song Two
Another community-written song, "Oh Precious," focuses on Jesus Christ and his finished work on the cross.

Song Three
A hymn, "Christ the Solid Rock," is done fairly traditionally. This is usually a transitional

point in the song worship so people can become more meditative. The music loops start to slip out and the video animation on the center screen slows down.

Song Four
A chorus by Stewart Townsend, "In Christ Alone," is sung.

Corporate Prayer Time
Light piano music to "In Christ Alone" continues to play in the background as the community prays. At the end of the corporate prayer time, the community stands (piano still playing) for a Scripture reading and an old Puritan prayer.

Back into Song Four
After the reading, everyone stands together and the community again joins in a unified confession by singing the last verse and chorus of "In Christ Alone."

Sermon
Every sermon begins with a reminder to people of why we study God's Word and how it is an act of worship. Before any Bibles are opened, a statement of belief is read in unity: "We believe that the Bible is the Word of God, fully inspired and without error in the original manuscripts, written under the inspiration of the Holy Spirit, and that it has supreme authority in all matters of faith and conduct." Bibles are provided for those who do not have them; they are spread all over the room for people to keep. People are also provided with an outline of the message so they can follow along. On the outline is a deeper study guide for individuals and groups to use. The sermon is usually about forty to 50 minutes long.

Song Five
A hymn, "O the Passion," is sung.

Prayer of Declaration
The worship song leader leads this time. The goal is to edify the body. The congregation holds hands as a sign of unity and prays the prayer of declaration out loud.

Song Six
Another community-written song, "Praise Arise," is sung.

You will notice The Gathering does not have a segment for announcements or offering. Announcements are usually done in the sermon if it fits. People can give their tithe any time during the worship or when entering or exiting the service. Offerings are placed in wooden boxes that look very rustic and are placed in different stations throughout the auditorium.

CHAPTER 12

Creating Multi-Congregational Worship Gatherings

Of all the new worship gatherings I've seen started within existing churches, those that have become multi-congregational worship gatherings have experienced the most freedom and empowerment. The multi-congregational approach has a lot of advantages, including the longer-term success of its leadership structures and strategies.

Several Worshiping Congregations in One Church

Multi-congregational worship gatherings see themselves as one church with distinct worshiping communities within them. The word "congregation" means assembly or gathering. It is possible for a single church to consist of several congregations.

These congregations within a church meet for distinct worship gatherings in response to cultural distinctions and differing styles of worship. Each congregation has its own pastor, staff, and leadership teams who understand the particular culture of the people they shepherd.

Each new congregation is birthed much like a church plant is and is somewhat autonomous. The difference is they are not designed to split off from the existing church. Some churches have launched new congregations that meet on different campuses, but they still see themselves as one church. Other churches have folded another congregation into their church, usually with a distinct culture (ethnic or emerging generations). The latter breathes new life into the original church, which otherwise might eventually die out.

In most cases, churches form multi-congregational worship gatherings because they sense change is needed if they are to engage the post-Christian emerging generations of their community. They decide to start a new worship gathering and ministry as a way of doing this. They might not specifically call themselves "multi-congregational," but the term will be used for the purposes of this book.

This chapter focuses on new congregations birthed with worship gatherings designed for emerging generations who grew up without a Judeo-Christian worldview. We'll now focus on a church that is moving in a good direction with this concept: Twin Lakes Church in Aptos, California.

1. Why a new worship gathering was needed at Twin Lakes Church

If you visit Twin Lakes Church, you'll discover a large church with extraordinary amounts of energy, life, and joy. It is a thriving Baptist church with a senior pastor who is a very gifted communicator and uses a lot of humor in his preaching. The senior pastor's leadership style is essentially communal, which makes for a healthy staff. The worship services are crowded, very contemporary, and lively with a lot of conversion growth.

However, Twin Lakes Church's leadership noticed that as the church's high school students graduated, they were increasingly disappearing from church. They tried to build a more traditional "college ministry" to solve this, but it did not turn out as they had hoped.

> "Whenever the method of worship becomes more important than the Person of worship, we have already prostituted our worship. There are entire congregations who worship praise and praise worship but who have not yet learned to praise and worship God in Jesus Christ."
> —Judson Cornwall

In a traditional college ministry, after all, the young adults are still part of the main worship services. The desire for a different form of worship gathering grew.

Twin Lakes Church wanted to develop a ministry geared to post-Christians growing up without a Judeo-Christian mindset. Up to that point, Twin Lakes was primarily seeing conversion growth among those with a modern mindset in the Baby Boomer population. They desired to broaden their scope of impact.

The Importance of Planning for Future Generations

Another important reason Twin Lakes Church wanted to start a new worship gathering was because they were looking ahead. Twin Lakes Church had one pastor for more than 50 years. The church aged right along with him. The format remained basically the same all those years. Slowly, that worship approach was alienating younger generations.

A great percentage of the original church members' children (who were Baby Boomers) left the church when they grew up. They were looking for forms of worship they were in tune with. This caused a good-sized exodus of younger people from the church. Eventually, the current senior pastor was hired. He brought a lot of life, energy, and creativity. He reconnected with Baby Boomers and the church was reborn in many ways.

The church's leadership looked ahead to the future and recognized that as the Baby Boomers aged, the same good-sized exodus scenario could happen again. They not only had emerging generations to think about, but they also saw cultural shifts taking place.

2. How the worship gathering functions in the whole church

Twin Lakes Church took a long time to think and pray through their next steps. Eventually, "Genesis" was birthed as a new worship gathering in the church.

Genesis meets on Sunday mornings at 10:30 during the same time one of the other main worship gatherings of the church meets (in order to share the children's ministry).

Genesis is not called a "young adult" worship gathering. No age labels are used to describe it. They call themselves the "fourth worship service" of the church. By its nature and worship forms, however, the Genesis gathering is primarily composed of those in their twenties.

Even though the worship gathering consists of a much younger community, Genesis is just as important as any other worship service in the church. Not labeling it as an age group or life-stage service validates it as a worship gathering. This takes away the sub-ministry stigma that many "young adult" worship gatherings have to deal with. Some teenagers go to Genesis. Much older people can also go to Genesis without feeling that they don't belong.

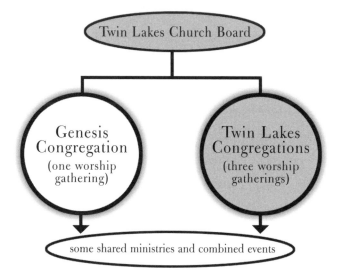

The strategy of this new worship gathering is not to funnel people into the other worship gatherings at Twin Lakes Church when people hit a certain age. Those who are part of the Genesis congregation will grow older together. They will be part of the church as a whole, but remain distinct as a congregation.

Because Genesis mainly consists of people in their twenties, the Genesis pastor oversees the young adult ministries of Twin Lakes Church. The church has young married, college, and post-college ministries. Individuals within Genesis serve as leaders of these life-stage ministries.

These life-stage ministries are designed for the entire church, not just Genesis. In fact, because the worship at Genesis is very different from the other worship services of Twin Lakes Church, individuals in both the college-age and career age ministries who don't resonate with Genesis go to the other worship services instead.

3. How the leadership is structured in the whole church

The pastor of Genesis reports to the senior pastor of Twin Lakes Church. The senior pastor is passionate about seeing emerging generations become part of a worshiping community. He doesn't exercise any sense of control or demonstrate any desire to be known within the congregation. So far, he has spoken at Genesis only once since it began.

Instead of having Genesis represented by the senior pastor (or someone else) to the board/elders of a church, they have the Genesis pastor at every board meeting (at this church, they don't have elder meetings, but board meetings as an equivalent). This way the Genesis pastor is there to personally represent the ministry and congregation of Genesis to the board. This makes a huge difference, as merely passing information is not an effective way to represent something. Especially with something as new and different as emerging worship gatherings and a new congregation are. It is critical that those in the highest level of leadership hear the heart, the passions, the "whys" behind something. In terms of leadership, the Genesis pastor and staff are also part of regular staff meetings in the church, so communication and a sense of oneness flows all the time in the relationship between the congregations.

4. What a Genesis worship gathering looks like

Walking into a Sunday-morning Genesis worship gathering, immediately there is the noticeable difference in that the lights are dim. The Genesis worship gathering meets in a multipurpose room that has to be set up and taken down each weekend. This limits the extent of what they can permanently do.

The first thing you see when you walk into the foyer is a large wooden cross set up dead center where the foyer ends and the main room opens up. The cross has cloth draped

"Who will not fear you, O Lord, and bring glory to your name? For you alone are holy. All nations come and worship before you, for your righteous acts have been revealed."
—Revelation 15:4

over it and candles at its base. This cross is unapologetically central to the reason they meet. The foyer also has a table with information about getting connected to other aspects of the Genesis community as well as the whole church.

Setting Up the Room as a Tabernacle

The room itself is set up to have a "tabernacle" feel to it. Black curtains are placed around most of the edges of the room, creating a circular feel. They use a lot of tables for people to sit at and several rows of chairs circling the stage area.

The rear corners of the room have prayer stations and tables. Each corner has a large tapestry. One tapestry has a large picture of Jesus' pierced hand painted on it. The other tapestry has a large picture of Jesus' face created out of mosaic tiles. People can kneel or sit on pillows placed in these corners.

Urns on every table give people a place to put prayer requests and offerings. These tables also are set up for communion.

The stage is set in the front of the room. They also have built an extended lower platform where the speaking and other leading takes place. They don't want to spotlight those up front, but bring them into the people as much as they can.

Sometimes they set up the band and worship leader on the side of the room. Most of the time, they lead up front sitting on stools.

The stage has black curtains behind it. Artwork created by members of the congregation hangs as a backdrop behind the stage. Hanging cloth sets off the sides of the stage where two pillars with candles form the shape of the cross.

Ending with a Question Instead of Ending with a Neat Wrap-Up

As for the flow of a worship gathering, they have a basic order where they start with a formal call to worship by reading Scripture out loud. They then have a time of worship music and community singing. They have announcements, but they call it "Community Time" where they try their best to express how to be involved in community, not just give out information about activities and events. The message lasts about 30 minutes. During both the message and the musical worship, they use PowerPoint® on a single screen that shows artwork and various graphics that match the atmosphere and vibe of the Genesis congregation.

Genesis concludes each message with a question. The question is a response to the message in terms of how it affects our daily worship of God and living in community. The question might be, "What am I depending on to transform my life — God's grace or my efforts?"

This goes against a lot of modern forms of preaching and teaching, as the usual ending is three or four clean-cut application points. Ending with a question moves people to wrestle with and ponder what was taught. Also, the message doesn't end the worship gathering. Instead, they then go into a longer time of worship, which is very important.

Responsive Worship

After the message comes a 30-minute time of responsive worship. This time includes singing, prayer, silence, and other responses. One time, the message was on our identity in Christ. The worship leader literally stopped the musical worship, put down his guitar, and led the people out of the room. They all went outside and took a community prayer walk around the church campus. Preplanned Scripture verses were posted on the walls so people could stop and read about their identity in Christ. It was a silent walk. They eventually made their way back to the meeting room where they broke into prayer groups to pray for one another.

Once, instead of singing or praying after the message, they set up tables where people wrapped gifts and baskets of clothing and food for the poor and elderly in the community. Another time they set up the stations of the cross symbolically using artwork sewed by members of the Genesis congregation. The worship time consisted of walking

"Worship is the believer's response of all that he is-- mind, emotions, will, and body-- to all that God is and says and does. This response has its mystical side in subjective experience, and its practical side in objective obedience to God's revealed truth. It is a loving response that is balanced by the fear of the Lord, and it is a deepening response as the believer comes to know God better." —Warren W. Wiersbe around and reading the Scriptures at each station.

Genesis also uses open microphones to allow community members to share their worship responses.

5. Summary and closing thoughts

The most important thing Twin Lakes Church is doing is avoiding the life-stage worship gathering approach. From the start, they have been focused on the mindset approach. They acknowledge that everyone in their twenties does not resonate with the Genesis worship gathering. This is fine with the leadership. It is understood that Genesis is for those who desire to worship God in a different form than the church's other gatherings.

Another thing that Genesis has which is critical is that the Genesis pastor is part of the board/elder meetings and he is seen with respect and not as a life-stage sort of pastor in terms of his role in the church. This seems critical to me, if they truly are equating these worship gatherings with the other ones in the church. I do wonder if there should be further elders or board members who are part of the new congregation in addition to the one pastor. This way there is a plurality of leadership to the congregation, as well as more than one voice in the board/elder meeting.

I look forward to seeing what happens in the future for Genesis, especially in how they develop the congregation's children's ministry. They currently do not incorporate children in the worship gatherings. Genesis allows parents to bring children in if they want to, but nothing in the gathering is designed with children specifically in mind. With some values shifting in the emerging church, children's ministry will be a central discussion on how spiritual formation works in a family. Typically children can be incorporated into at least part of worship gatherings. This issue needs to be considered further.

Overall, the multi-congregational approach seems to be the most effective way for a church to start a worship gathering and community for emerging generations. By doing this, they have far fewer worries since they share facilities for maximum Kingdom benefit. They can combine for all-church events and share certain ministries. They also aren't grappling with trying to shift people from one worship gathering to another at a certain age.

The key to this is the empowerment and freedom the Twin Lakes senior pastor and leadership have given to the Genesis pastor and other congregational leaders. I pray more existing church leaders will follow their example to empower leadership for emerging generations. This can make or break multi-congregational worship gatherings in the long run, and we can learn from Twin Lakes Church and Genesis' wonderful example of not being afraid to experiment like this.

Sample Worship Gathering

Genesis at Twin Lakes Church

Call to Worship
Genesis gatherings start with a Scripture reading to focus attention on the reason of the meeting.

Musical Worship
The choruses "Here I Am to Worship" and "Better Is One Day" are sung. Graphics are used on the screens through the musical worship. The band maintains a low profile, often sitting on stools so attention is not focused on them.

Community Life
Announcements are presented as ways for people to become part of the community. As a result, this part of the gathering is called "Community Life," not "Announcements."

Message
A 30-minute message is given while graphics are shown on the screens. Sometimes interactive questions are included as part of the message. The message always ends with a question.

Music/Communion/Offering
The next section of the gathering is where people respond to the message and the question asked while musical worship continues. They are allowed to walk around the worship space,

take communion from the tables, give offering in urns at the corners of the room, write out prayer requests, and turn them in to baskets by a cross. People can respond in worship in whatever form they may want to, and each week is a little different in the prayer stations or whatever else they may set up. There may be communal readings of Scripture or communal prayer during this time. The songs they sing include "Enough," "God of Wonders," "Everything," "Jesus You're Everything," "Beside Me," and "Agnus Dei."

Prayer and Send-Off

CHAPTER 13

Starting a New Kind of Church

This chapter tells a little about my personal story. It covers our journey with the Graceland worship gathering at Santa Cruz Bible Church in Santa Cruz, California. We experimented with some of the same approaches discussed in the previous three chapters. In our setting, we ended up evolving and morphing to the point of starting a new kind of church: Vintage Faith Church.

1. Why a new worship gathering was needed

For years we had a large high school ministry at Santa Cruz Bible Church. We used modern outreach methodology — lots of drama, videos, pop-rock music, and the usual big youth ministry programming. This approach of ministry went on for several years fairly successfully. That is, until we began sensing a cultural change happening among youth. This contemporary approach to youth ministry was losing its effectiveness for non-churched teens. We weren't alone in noticing this trend. All across the country, youth leaders were realizing that teenagers outside the church were developing an increasingly non-Judeo-Christian worldview.

This cultural change caused us to rethink our approach youth ministry. We had designed our ministry for teenagers with a Judeo-Christian worldview and for teens who had been strongly influenced by it (even if they were self-proclaimed atheists). We realized we now needed to design a new ministry for people with a postmodern, post-Christian worldview.

As missionaries, we began rethinking evangelism, worship gatherings, spiritual formation, how we taught Scripture. This rethinking eventually moved beyond youth ministry—since the youth ministry is shaped by the church it's a part of—to rethinking church.

Vintage Christianity and Worship for Youth

Slowly but surely, we began experimenting. We shifted many of our values. We began talking about Jesus and worshiping in the presence of unbelievers in a more unapologetic way in our youth meetings. We brought back a lot of the "spiritual" expressions of worship that had been removed. We still kept things very lively. Our youth ministry didn't turn into a silent monastery, but it definitely took a turn away from the high energy meetings we once had.

Instead of using lots of flash, videos, and music while trying to squeeze in a brief Bible message, we reversed the whole thing. We created a sacred space by using candles and crosses and other symbols. We still had upbeat times of worship in singing, but we also implemented times of quiet and contemplation. Very straightforward talks about Kingdom living and Jesus' teachings replaced burying the message behind videos, dramas, and other things.

This move to a rather raw and simplistic approach to ministry is vintage Christianity. The response was amazing! Non-Christian teenagers said, "I like this — this is spiritual."

Creating a *Vintage* *Young Adult Ministry*

Seeing the change that came from altering our approach in youth ministry, we wondered if this move to a vintage approach would have the same impact on "young adults" ages 18 and up.

At the time, we had a terrific main worship service at Santa Cruz Bible Church. It had fantastic preaching, tons of energy, and vibrancy. It was extremely contemporary and attracted a lot of people! But apart from those who grew up in the church, we weren't seeing too many people under the age of 30.

When I began dialoguing with young adults raised outside of the church, I found many of them were looking for something different in a church experience. Larger churches like ours embraced the values of excellence, tight programming, and very how-to and very biblical application-oriented preaching with the sermon serving as the focal point of the worship service. This was great for previous generations, but it was not resonating with new generations, who felt like they were simply sitting in a room where they sang a few songs (however contemporary they were) and mainly listened to the message (however great it was).

We decided to experiment. We stopped our traditional college ministry — which was basically a miniature version of the main services — and started an age-specific, young adult worship gathering called "Graceland" that met on Sunday nights. We not only rethought the worship gathering, but also how we approached spiritual formation. We began by building a strong base of home groups that met midweek. This is where people experienced community and had deeper Bible discussions.

Over the next two years, God blessed Graceland and it grew incredibly fast. People came to faith who had never been to church before. A lot of disillusioned Christians who had left the church now returned.

It was an exciting period of time. Yet a few issues popped up that needed to be addressed. I remember the extremely awkward time I had to tell someone he was over age

30 and couldn't stay. He said, "I am able to worship God here; why can't I be here?" Another time, I walked over to a couple of teenagers to tell them the same thing, but I stopped and couldn't do it. I watched those teenagers worshiping and couldn't help but wonder why they couldn't stay.

Having a worship gathering with set age limits created a strange and unnecessary dilemma. The reason we started Graceland was to reach those who weren't resonating with the modern approach to worship. For the most part, the people coming to Graceland didn't go to the main services because they didn't connect — regardless of their age.

The traditional approach of putting people in age-based meetings started messing up my head. I had never thought through life-stage approaches in terms of worship gatherings before.

I clearly understand that we need life-skill training for children, youth, college students, singles, pre-married couples, young married families, and other people in crucial life-stage situations. No question!

But what about worship gatherings? Are we supposed to divide people up by life-stages yet again?

Should We Divide the Body and Family?

The more we thought about all this, the more unsettled we became. How did we come up with so many age-dividers in our churches? Isn't the church supposed to be a *body*? Then why do we often dissect the church body into little parts, rather than seeing it function holistically together?

Isn't the church supposed to be a *family*? Then why do we constantly separate families when they come to church meetings? It is interesting to think about. It's been said that Sunday morning at 11 is the most radically segregated hour; I wonder if it's the most age-segregated hour, too?

The two primary metaphors for the church as a body and a family break down when we gather as a church. It doesn't make sense!

Creating a Vintage All-Age Worship Gathering

After several discussions with our senior pastor at the time, Chip Ingram, we eventually turned Graceland into an all-age worship gathering and ministry. When we dropped the age limits and made it a worship gathering for any age, it grew even faster! We were no longer a life-stage ministry but a full-fledged worship gathering of the church. Probably 80 percent of the overall population of the gathering was still under 30 years of age. But we began to see a growing percentage of people over 30 who also resonated with this approach to worship.

Graceland met Sunday nights at six o'clock. As it grew, a second Graceland gathering was added at eight o'clock.

"This Place Is Diverse – with a Capital D"

God continued to do amazing things, and we saw all types of people drawn into the Graceland community. People who had never been to a church before came and many began trusting in Jesus. A van picked up runaway teens and others in downtown Santa Cruz and brought them to Graceland because they wanted to be there. Many unchurched teenagers who normally wouldn't be part of a traditional youth ministry were there. A lot of university students become part of Graceland; we even sent a bus to campus to pick them up. I remember some rather intense and loving discussions I had with those practicing different sexual lifestyles as we opened the Scriptures and talked through human sexuality. I remember so many conversations with people holding extreme religious beliefs as well.

Chip finally came to see what was going on in Graceland. He had never been there before, which showed he had a lot of trust in us to go that long without coming to see what we were doing!

He and I left the building together after the worship gathering ended. I asked him what he thought. I always will remember his comments to me. He said "This place is diverse—with a capital D." He commented that it was exciting for him to be there because it reminded him of the book of Acts.

The Big Questions Start Arising

It was a thrilling time, but we still had to grapple with questions about structure. We asked, "How does Graceland fit within the whole church? How does a church have a another worship community within it? Is this a church-within-a-church? Is this an alternative worship service? How do elders fit into Graceland?"

It was messy! We didn't know what to do. Historically, church ministry functioned in a certain way and there was a specific approach to looking at the church leadership structure. But Graceland started going against the norms of consistency and church uniformity! What do we do?

Detours and Wrong Roads

We began a lot of discussions since Graceland now had become a major part of the church. There was a desire to make things cleaner and more aligned all around. Eventually we decided to integrate Graceland into the values and systems of Santa Cruz Bible Church. We aligned the preaching, for instance, thinking that would bring Graceland into conformity with the rest of the church's teaching.

We divided up the staff to form all-church teams according to function, rather than having specific teams for Graceland. Josh Fox, who led Graceland's worship, became part of the Santa Cruz Bible Church worship team. I became part of the Santa Cruz Bible Church teaching team.

On paper, this looked great and made sense! But in reality, we learned some big lessons.

The more we aligned the values and infrastructure and style of leadership of

Graceland and Santa Cruz Bible Church, however, the more we distanced ourselves from the very things that made Graceland unique. Instead of our discussions being exciting ones about mission and innovation, they turned into discussions about squeezing Graceland into how the rest of the church functioned.

Graceland suddenly felt wrong. We saw fewer and fewer of whom I would consider post-Christian people coming and more and more already-Christians with a modern mindset. In many ways it wasn't Graceland anymore. We slowly but surely became a miniature version of what already was happening in the other worship services and the rest of the church.

So, once again we began having discussions.

We recognized that moving Graceland into alignment with the rest of the church wasn't quite working like we thought it would. There were clashes in small-group values, in membership values.

What we lost most at Graceland was the distinct leadership community. We had different approaches to and different values of leadership, and when that was changed, it was a really, really big deal. We recognized that spiritual formation for post-Christian culture is going to look, feel, and be different than modern culture.

All missionaries who engage other cultures know the first thing to do is learn that culture's value systems and philosophies rather than pushing their own values and philosophies. That's what happened when we thought Graceland was only going to change in terms of music (and maybe a few candles). No, it was about a philosophical and value-system change that went way beyond just the worship gathering.

Recognizing where we had gone astray, we decided to go back to our original vision—but began talking about birthing a new church instead of simply trying to "fix" what we broke.

2. How the worship gathering functions in the whole church

As we further explored the options of launching a new church, we decided that it would not be the best stewardship of finances and facilities to keep Graceland going and also start Vintage Faith Church. Graceland wasn't quite the same as it used to be and needed a rebirthing.

So, we made a rather drastic move and ended the Graceland worship gatherings for more than two months. This gave us a few months to retrain those who wanted to be part of the new church. We needed to deconstruct and de-program people's thinking and expectations about church and retrain them about the philosophy of a missional church.

We started Vintage Faith Church and sort of morphed Graceland into both Santa Cruz Bible Church and Vintage Faith Church. Our first weekend worship gathering took place on a Sunday night on the Santa Cruz Bible Church campus — at the same time and place Graceland had met. We selected elders from the Graceland community to become part of the Santa Cruz Bible Church elder board and be trained to serve as Vintage Faith Church elders. Instead of becoming a traditional church plant, we became two sister-hybrid churches.

Sharing Certain Ministries as Two Churches for Greater Impact

We started asking more questions. Which of our two ministries' values and philosophies match up? Which ones don't? What things need to be distinctly separate as two churches, and what can be done together as two churches? Where things could be done together, we did so! Where things didn't match up, we remained distinct churches.

As it is structured now, it is the best of both worlds and the best for maximum Kingdom impact. After all the wondering and evolution we went through, I never would have guessed it would happen this way. Yet it makes perfect sense to accelerate the Kingdom impact a local church can have, not by starting an entirely new church, but by starting a sister-hybrid-church and remaining in close relationship. In a way, it takes the multi-congregational model to the next level.

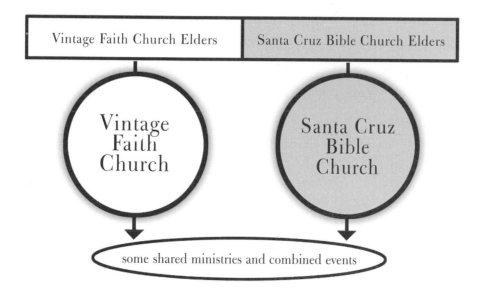

| Vintage Faith Church Elders | Santa Cruz Bible Church Elders |

Vintage Faith Church

Santa Cruz Bible Church

some shared ministries and combined events

"But if an unbeliever or someone who does not understand comes in while everybody is prophesying, he will be convinced by all that he is a sinner and will be judged by all, and the secrets of his heart will be laid bare. So he will fall down and worship God, exclaiming, 'God is really among you!'"
—I Corinthians 14:24-25

3. How the leadership is structured in the whole church

The elders of Vintage Faith Church meet with the Santa Cruz Bible Church elders as needed to keep the big picture in mind. The Vintage Faith Church elders also meet on their own regularly for specific Vintage Faith Church shepherding and church business. We function as two churches, but stay close to accelerate Kingdom impact in our community.

I currently meet weekly with the primary leadership team of Santa Cruz Bible Church both for accountability and for discussing the bigger picture outlook for Santa Cruz County. Our staffs are even planning on doing some joint events. If two churches see themselves as "family," it should be only natural to have family functions and do things together.

Emerging Worship Gatherings Designed to Be Part of the Holistic Church

As we moved to form a new sister-hybrid church, we needed to start with some new philosophical values. This was a huge lesson we learned about becoming truly missional in our culture. It involved rethinking far more than what happens in a worship gathering.

These philosophical values show not only what the emerging worship gathering would be like, but, more importantly, how the new worship gathering fits within the holistic plan for spiritual formation.

Setting values for an emerging church and emerging worship holistically is important to think through! In our context, here are some of the philosophical values we have focused on:

- **We desire to do things that happen and can be explained only by the Holy Spirit's involvement, not by our use of innovative ministry methodology.**
  - Prayer is the base for all we do, not something we squeeze in (John 15).
  - The Spirit-filled life (Romans 6-8) is our source of strength and life change and is understood by everyone.

- **We desire to be a church that is a mission, not a church that has a missions "department."**
  - Our mission is to invite others to join us as disciples of Jesus as we abandon our self-centeredness and experience the saving grace of Jesus and the love of God. We express this through acts of love, kindness, service, social justice, and blessing to others.
  - Missions cannot be compartmentalized and seen as "over there somewhere." We see all members of Vintage Faith Church as local missionaries. We strive to have the same zeal and excitement in our daily lives that we have overseas on missions trips.
  - We see social justice as part of our mission both locally and globally (Micah 6:8).

- **We will be an equipping church. The Vintage Faith Church staff empowers people of the church to fulfill their God-given dreams and ministries.**

- The staff's primary role is to train and equip believers for the mission (Ephesians 4:12).

- The staff maintains a culture that allows people to begin ministries. People are encouraged to be involved in ministries that match who they are and what their dreams are, not just to fill needed ministry slots.

- **We will ruthlessly ensure that it is clearly known that "the church is the people" and that "you can't go to church."**

  - We teach and embody the truth of Romans 12:1-2. The disciples of Jesus worship God with a daily sacrificial lifestyle; worship doesn't happen when we sing or when we all meet.

  - We have a network of smaller communities that gather in homes and other places during the week. Each weekend, we all meet together in a large group for a community gathering.

  - We make sure that the large weekend gathering is not thought of as the "church" to avoid a consumeristic expectation.

- **We will be extremely passionate about developing a church culture that promotes and provides deep theological training.**

  - We desire to teach the whole of Scripture deeply as we learn to worship and love God with our heart, mind, and strength (Matthew 22:37). We don't strive for information, but for heart transformation and for equipping for the mission of making disciples.

  - Because we are on a mission, we provide intense Bible training, apologetics classes, and theology classes to support and fuel our missionary skills and passion (Hebrews 5:11-6:3). We desire to encourage and teach people to think and ask questions and dialogue.

- **We will build this church as a family church, breaking down the departmental separation of families within the church structure as much as possible.**
  - The church worship gatherings are designed to incorporate children in part, in addition to the children's ministries designed for them.
  - As often as we can, we desire to have families worship together.
  - We are strong in training parents to be the primary spiritual leaders of their children and to not depend solely on the church (Deuteronomy 6:4-8).
  - We establish intergenerational mentoring relationships to allow the older generations to impart wisdom to the younger.

- **We will use the creative arts to an extreme in all we do, combining the ancient with the future in worship and on a mission.**
  - In our weekend worship gatherings, we combine the beauty and richness of ancient liturgy and our Jewish roots with our current local culture expressions of worship.
  - We aim to fully reflect the creativity of God in our worship gatherings and in the lifeblood of all we do (Genesis 1, Exodus 31:3-5).
  - We use creativity and the arts to become an active part of the Santa Cruz County community at large and to glorify God through expressing creativity in whatever we do (1 Corinthians 10:31).

These are some of the values we have shaping Vintage Faith Church, which is important because from the holistic outlook we then see how the worship gathering fits in (not visa versa). The worship gathering is but one part of things, not the central part. We are building not from the large weekend worship gathering, but from the church being the church throughout the week and meeting in community in smaller settings as their primary community. Then we all meet on the weekend together.

"To worship God in truth is to recognize Him for being who He is, and to recognize ourselves for what we are."
—Brother Lawrence

We also are developing an intensive Bible and theological training center to teach in a different environment than in a large meeting and lecture format. Our goal is to use the most effective approaches to see Scripture and theology remembered and then lived out in relationships.

A lot of things happen outside our worship gathering, so focusing primarily on the worship gathering is not how we have birthed Vintage Faith Church.

Being in the Cultural Hub with the People

As this book is written, we are looking in downtown Santa Cruz for a space to open a coffeehouse, art gallery, cyber-café, music venue, and office space. Although we have our large weekend worship gatherings on the Santa Cruz Bible Church campus and at various other spaces, we desire our base of operation to be among the people. Downtown Santa Cruz is our cultural hub. It is where everyone hangs out and is a very active place. So instead of setting up offices in the suburbs, we want to participate in the local downtown community as salt and light (Matthew 5:13-16).

The Vintage Faith Church offices and coffeehouse will be known for what they are. We won't leave tracts on the tables or have coffee cups with Bible verses on them. We won't try to be a "Christian coffeehouse" where all the Christians hang out. Instead, we will strive to spread Kingdom influence through the conversations, art, music, and poetry that will be part of this venue.

4. What a Vintage Faith Church gathering looks like

When you walk into a Vintage Faith Church worship gathering, the lights are dimmed. At a greeting table people are ready to say hello and answer questions. Information is available in various pamphlets for people to learn about the church and about getting involved in our worship community.

Some people serve our church community by wandering about welcoming people as they would welcome family members who have come for dinner (or as a friend of a family member if they are new).

Crosses and other Christian symbols are on the tables to immediately communicate that this is a sacred space where we worship and follow Jesus.

The room has black curtains set up around the edges to make the room more circular. The curtains also create natural spaces behind them for prayer stations that aren't in everyone's direct view. We originally set up the curtains for aesthetic purposes only, but people ended up going behind them for prayer. A mix of tables and chairs creates a communal living room rather than a performance or theatre on the black curtains. Art created by people in our church community hangs on black curtains. Sometimes if we are doing a thematic series in the teaching, the artists create new art to coincide with that. Candles are on the tables as well as scattered in places around the room to invoke a sense of reverence and that something special is happening here.

Prayer stations, which may or may not tie into the teaching of the evening, are set up for people to journal prayers and thoughts. People also are free to paint at various art stations. Some stations have pillows and a cross for people to pray. Some stations may have thematic meaning to them, with Scriptures and props communicating the truths of Scripture, which people can touch and interact with somehow.

As people walk into the room, they see screens with art and images and sometimes Scriptures projected on them. Images projected on the sides of the room show ancient architecture and other images that remind us how old Christianity is (it's not something modern).

A low stage is set up in the front of the room, where some speaking occurs, but the stage is also projected out into where the people sit and is not a centerpiece. Other low stages to the side and rear of the room are used by the worship band and choir. The worship leading and choir are out of the direct view for the most part, to avoid putting the focus on them.

Keeping Jesus as the Centerpiece of the Gathering

The creative décor is an attempt to signify that Jesus is the center of our meeting. Crosses are in the front of the room with the screens. When worship happens, the view of the cross represents the risen Jesus. During communion, the tables holding the bread and cup become the centerpiece of the room, again showing that Jesus is the center of all we do. The space consistently reflects Jesus as the focus — not the bands, speakers, artwork, or candles — only Jesus.

Keeping Worship Gatherings as Family-Oriented as Possible

To formally start the worship gathering, a reading of Scripture or a welcome occurs, then perhaps a few celebratory songs of worship. Some community direction is then given by someone who tells how to be connected in community and tells about other ways to experience what it means to be a disciple of Jesus. Children are encouraged to be in the worship gathering up to the teaching part, where we then dismiss them into appropriate children's classes. We are scheduling periodic worship gatherings that will incorporate children into the whole thing so they can be with their families.

We also incorporate teenagers into the worship gatherings, so they understand this is for them and is not just the "adults'" place to be. After many years as a youth pastor, I think it is critical to focus more on spiritual formation in youth ministry and not duplicate large worship gatherings, but instead incorporate youth and families into them.

Teaching Kingdom Living as Disciples of Jesus

After the community announcements, a variety of things happen. There may be a reflective Scripture reading, a video loop of images behind the lyrics of a worship song, and a communal reading of a prayer or creed. At some point we move into the time for teaching. The teaching occurs from a lower stage that extends into where people sit rather than from a higher platform.

The teaching time is around 25 to 35 minutes. We use large sections of Scripture to tell the story of God and how we can be living as disciples of Jesus. This theo-topical teaching is God-centered (versus man-centered) and encourages the church to be living as disciples of Jesus who are inviting others into Kingdom living and serving others. We strongly encourage people to bring Bibles to the gathering, and many Bibles are given away if people need them.

The teaching usually includes a look at the historical meaning and the Jewish roots of the Scriptures. More often than not, we use props to communicate and invite people to response. We use a lot of visuals—artwork, photography, and other images — and Scripture quotations and key words on the screens during our teaching times.

We try to teach with depth since we believe emerging generations are hungering to learn the truths of Scripture and the story of the Bible. We elevate the usage of the Scriptures highly in these gatherings. We also recognize that the preaching that occurs in a large gathering is generally more short-term motivational and inspirational in nature, so we don't see or teach that it is the one weekly feeding people should have. Instead, we teach and help people learn to feed themselves and provide other teaching and training opportunities outside of the large worship gatherings. In our opinion, most longer-term learning and transformation happen relationally in other contexts, so we focus a lot of our energy outside the larger worship gatherings in that regard. We very strongly teach the Bible in our gatherings — but maybe not in the way the modern church views teaching and preaching.

An Example of a Message Given from Ephesians 2-3

During one teaching message, we read through Ephesians 2-3. We showed from 2:8-9 how we are saved by grace and that we are God's workmanship (his *poiema*), which he created for a purpose. We explained how a form of the word "workmanship" (*poiema*) is where we get the word "poem." We used the metaphor of how each of us is a beautiful poem, a piece of artistic workmanship that God created for a purpose. We read through Ephesians 3:10 and showed how God has chosen the church to display his manifold (multilayered, multicolored) wisdom. We showed on the screens photographs of stained glass images from a church that captured various biblical scenes. We showed a series of stained glass images from that same church that captured men and women throughout church history. We talked about the stained glass images as we showed them on the screens.

We showed one image of Augustine (AD 353-430) writing a book and next to him was a flaming heart. The book showed that his skill and talent for writing was used by God to capture beautiful words in books such as *The City of God*. The heart represented his heart aflame for Jesus. There were arrows through the heart, representing his remorse for his past sin.

We then showed a stained glass portrait of St. Boniface (AD 673-754), who was shown holding a large book with a sword in it and an ax in the other hand. The ax spoke of his work as a pastor in Germany, where he took a stand against people who worshiped spirits in trees and by cutting down a tree and building a chapel with the wood, demonstrating there is only one true God. The book with the sword showed that Boniface was martyred. As he was being killed, he held a commentary on the Bible high in the air to keep it from being damaged from the swords as they struck him.

We showed another stained glass image of Bach (AD 1685-1750) playing an organ for God's glory, with the letters "SDG" next to him. These letters, which Bach often put on his the musical manuscripts he wrote, stand for *Soli Deo Gloria* (Latin for "Glory to God Alone").

We showed a few other stained glass images and explained how each of these men and women from church history were remembered in a certain way because of what they did with their lives. Each of them was an imperfect sinner saved by grace, but God used them for his glory. We explained how we all are stained (with sin), but it is the light of Jesus Christ shining through us that brings brilliance to the stained glass. We made the analogy that the stained glass pieces themselves, without being put together to form a picture, are rather drab pieces of glass.

They are beautiful only when they are assembled and the sunlight comes through them.

We then raised the question: What would our stained glass image look like? What will we be remembered for? How can God use us, saved by grace, to allow the light of Jesus Christ to shine through us? We drew an example of what a personal stained glass image could look like and then we asked everyone there to think of what they would like to see their stained glass image be like. What symbols would they want to be remembered for?

Contemplative Musical Worship, Prayer, and Meditation

After that message from Ephesians 2-3, we then began another more contemplative musical worship time, where people got out of their chairs and picked up paper and crayons and pens and went around the room to draw portraits of their stained glass or what they would want it to look like. People were able to pray, reread the Ephesians passage, think, and draw.

The worship music was deliberately more contemplative during this post-teaching time. Usually after teaching we also use some Taize-like songs (Scriptures sung in somewhat of a harmonic chant) and some slower pop worship songs. The choir sings from the side of the room or rear of the room. The choir either backs up the band or sings ancient choral songs so people could simply pause and listen and pray.

During this music time, people found spaces all around the room to draw symbols, write words, and pray that God would use them for his purpose as part of the church. After they were done, they pinned their drawings onto a wall where everyone could see them "on display" (Ephesians 3:10).

The evening continued with more singing and an offering time where bags were passed around for people to put in prayer requests and financial offerings. Then we closed with a benediction and wrapup to bless the people and challenge them to go out on the mission God had created them for.

Please see my first book, *The Emerging Church,* for more about multisensory worship gatherings, including many examples of what we and other churches have done in that realm.

Using Multisensory Elements in Worship

Sometimes the offering is taken from tables with lit incense to symbolize our offerings going up before the throne as incense. Other times, people write prayers on cards and pin them to a prayer wall. Or people exchange prayer cards and take home someone else's card in order that we can pray for one another.

Sometimes we ask for people to pray with others, or sit and pray alone if they wish. We always make sure we don't force people to participate in something. We give permission for people to sit and observe if they wish, so they don't feel awkward.

We might include pauses for communal prayers or readings of creeds. We might have directed times of silence. We may have a time of open sharing where people express sentence prayers or words out loud. We might have Scripture readings before specific songs. We might have someone tell the story behind a hymn before we sing it. Someone may have a poem to read. Someone may have an art piece to explain. It all depends on the gathering. We plan ahead, but we still allow the Holy Spirit to move and change anything we may have planned.

Once a month right now, we have communion evenings with a shorter teaching time so the whole evening revolves around communion. We set it up in various ways, sometimes in the front, sometimes in the center of the room, sometimes around the room. We have Scriptures that people read on the tables as they come forward to take the communion after we've explained its meaning.

We spend a lot more energy and time designing the communion nights. The other weeks are still very multisensory in terms of worship, but with communion we have extended times of prayer at stations or with each other or however it is done that night. The big thing is not to get burned out and get too caught up in programming or trying to top each week with something better. That is a bad cycle to enter! So we lessen things for the weeks we aren't taking communion in terms of effort we put into all the creativity.

We don't want to teach people that worship is all about being multisensory. Instead, we teach people that transformation takes place in their lives as disciples. What we give to God in worship is what is important, not whether we have art and candles. If we are not helping people become more Christlike, then we are merely putting on an entertaining show, not worshiping. Worship should change us, not make us feel good or entertain us. Again, it is not about us — it is about Jesus.

5. Summary and closing thoughts

When Graceland first started as a worship gathering within Santa Cruz Bible Church, I imagined it would keep going as it was for the next 20 years. We had no plans to ever go through so many changes and become a church. But you know God is active when things go differently than you planned!

The New Testament Is Full of Change and the Early Church Was Never Stagnant

When I read through the New Testament, I see that things were always changing. Who would have guessed that people would move from the Temple to homes in order to worship? Who would have guessed that a persecutor of Christians named Saul would become the apostle Paul? Who would have guessed all the fascinating twists and turns of events that occurred in the church during the book of Acts?

So why should we not expect an exciting ride in today's church with all types of fascinating twists and turns of events? We should expect them!

I didn't always think like that, of course. I used to think that we should try to figure things out with a neat system of leadership and strategy and then stick to it no matter what. I have learned, however, especially in the emerging church and with our fast-changing emerging culture, that we had better not only get used to changes and twists, but enjoy and embrace them.

I also now believe that if a church remains the same too long, then the Holy Spirit may not be at work in it! When the Holy Spirit is involved in the church, he moves as he wants and directs things as Jesus, the head of the church, sees fit. That is why we need to stick close to him in dependency and in prayer, so we know what he wants us to do.

Bridging Two Worlds of Two Types of Churches

With Vintage Faith Church, we are trying to build a bridge between a modern contemporary church (Santa Cruz Bible Church) and an emerging church (Vintage Faith Church). I pray that many more churches will try to creatively come up with ways to bridge churches during this cultural transition. There is so much potential for good if modern and traditional churches are willing to build bridges and birth emerging churches and emerging worship gatherings. I pray that ego and control issues won't get in the way of what God can do in bridging churches and extending the diversity of a church's mission.

I recently heard of an older church on the verge of dying out that decided to allow a younger pastor and a new church plant he was leading to come in and bring new life to their church. They still have a morning worship gathering where the older people in the church worship and this younger pastor teaches them. But his church plant now meets there on Sunday nights. What a beautiful demonstration of Kingdom values this shows!

Vintage Faith Church is designed to have its own elders and to be financially independent of Santa Cruz Bible Church. Vintage Faith Church is not considered a glorified sub-ministry of sorts, but a viable church in its own right. This changes how we view ourselves and our ability to make decisions according to our specific philosophical values.

To me, it seems the best of both worlds right now. During this transition, it's a way for two types of churches to stay in relationship, for generations to stay connected, but for churches to still be who they need to be independently for their specific missions. We have plans with Santa Cruz Bible Church to launch more churches and to develop a ministry training center bringing all the churches together. Plenty of adventure is still ahead and we shall see where Jesus leads us next!

Sample Worship Gathering

Vintage Faith Church

Theme for Gathering

Understanding how much God loves us: a look at what it means to be the Bride of Christ.

Walk-in Music

We play a techno CD mix.

Scriptures on the Screens

As people walk in, the screens show the Scriptures that will be taught during the meeting. The Scripture has art background and loops on the screen until the gathering formally begins.

Worship Music

Band plays from side stage, out of direct view. Lyrics are on screens with art and stained glass backgrounds. Songs include "Open the Eyes of My Heart," "Lord, Let Your Glory Fall," and "Revelation."

Scripture Reading

Someone reads Colossians 1:15-20.

Worship Music

We sing "The Breastplate of St. Patrick Prayer" (a song our musical worship leader, Josh Fox, wrote using the St. Patrick Prayer).

Community Announcements

Welcome and various ways to become connected in the Vintage Faith community. Children are dismissed at this time to go to their classes.

Mingle Time

We give people a few minutes to greet one another.

Song

Josh Fox uses the song "I Can Only Imagine," a song by Mercy Me, to set up the evening's theme. As we sing, Scriptures and selected lyrics from the song appear on the screens.

Message

"What It Means to Be the Bride of Christ." Seven tables are set up among the people, each one heavily decorated with various teaching props. These tables serve as interactive prayer stations for people to visit. The 30-minute message explains the format of Jewish weddings in New Testament times. The message is given while standing next to each of the tables, pointing out the various props, and showing how metaphors from Jewish weddings relate to the church. Visuals on the screens show photographs of the things being talked about and the Scriptures being used.

Table 1: The Selection of the Bride—John 15:16 and 1 Peter 1:8-9

This table has a mirror on it and the words "He loves you and He chose you" written all around the edges of the table. It tells how a bride in New Testament times would be chosen by the groom's father, in the same way that God the Father has chosen us and what an awesome honor that is. The mirror is for people to see themselves as they go to the table and read the truth that they are chosen by God the Father. Despite who they think they are, or how inadequate the feel, as they see themselves in the mirror they are reminded that they have been especially selected and chosen by the Father to be part of the church, the Bride of Christ.

Table 2: The Bride Price (*mohar*) — 1 Corinthians 6:19-20

This table has a cross standing in the center of it as the main focus. Around the edges of the table are the words "He paid the price for you." Here we teach that after a bride was selected, the next step was to determine the price (*mohar*). The greater the price the groom's father paid, the greater the value placed on the bride. The metaphor here is that the ultimate price was paid to purchase the Bride of Christ, and that was the death of the groom. The passage about how we were bought for a price is read, reinforcing the truth that the Father must consider us of great worth to have paid such a high price. A painting of the crucifixion is on the screens as this is being taught.

Table 3: The Engagement Contract (*ketubah*) Listing Gifts for the Bride — 1 Corinthians 12:8-9, Romans 12, Ephesians 4

This table is set up with several props, including communion cups, bread, a Bible, and a contract listing a number of promised gifts: "eternal life, Holy Spirit, forgiveness, eternal life, faith, mercy, service, teaching," etc. It teaches how in a Jewish wedding, after the price was determined that the father would pay for the bride, a contract (*ketubah*) was drawn up. This contract listed the promises of gifts that the bride would receive. The bride then gave her consent, and they drank a glass of wine to seal this and set the bride apart. The deal was sealed when the wine was drunk and the contract was given to the bride, so she could hold the groom to the promises made. As the Bride of Christ, we are promised many gifts when we trust in Jesus. We have these promises in the Bible (our contract). When we take communion, we remember the sealed deal when we trusted in Jesus Christ. We also remember we have been "set apart" as his bride, just as a bride was set apart in New Testament times. The groom and bride were not yet joined in marriage, but their engagement was considered as seriously as if they were already married.

Table 4: Cleansing Water (*mikvah*)

This table is set up with bowls of water and towels. When people visit this station they wash their hands as a remembrance. Along the edges of the table is written "Remember your baptism or be baptized if you haven't." There is also a basket with cards and pencils for people to write their names and phone numbers and leave in the basket if they want to be baptized. This table teaches that after her engagement, a Jewish bride would take a ritual bath called a *mikvah*. We tie this into the Bride of Christ getting baptized in water as an outward sign of her commitment to Jesus Christ. On the screens we show archaeological ruins of *mikvahs* at the time of Jesus, as well as contemporary ones that look very much like our baptismals.

Table 5: The Groom Prepares the Wedding Chamber and We Await His Return — John 14:1-3, 1 Thessalonians 4:16, Matthew 25:13

This table has a ram's horn *shofar* in the center and the rest of the table is flooded with candles. In New Testament times, a groom went to his father's house after he was engaged to build an additional room. It was up to the father to tell his son when he should go fetch his bride. The groom then marched into town and blew a *shofar* to let everyone know he was now fetching her from her house and bringing her back to the room he had built in his father's house. This ties into how Jesus taught that he was going to his Father's house to prepare a place for us, his Bride, and that one day he would return to get us, but only his Father knows the time and date. Jesus also told us to keep watch for his return, so the candles represent the bridesmaids' lamps kept trimmed and burning while awaiting the return of the groom. Around the table are the words "Are you ready to meet the Groom?"

Table 6: The Wedding of The Groom and Bride Is Finalized — 1 Thessalonians 4:17 and 1 Peter 5:4

On this table are little cups of juice that everyone can take and drink. This represents how when the groom finally fetched the bride, they returned to the father's house. Sometimes a crown was placed on the bride for the final ceremony. They often also drank another cup of wine. This took place under an especially built canopy (*chupah*) built by the groom. They finalized the ceremony under this canopy. Sometime in ancient Jewish customs, the bride and groom smashed the glass they shared and drank from by stepping on it. This symbolized how their two lives were joined together. At this table we show that Jesus will one day fetch his bride, the Church, and they will go to the Father's house together. When people come to this station they read around the edge of the table "He loves you and will commit to you." There is a canopy built next to this station and underneath it people drink from a little plastic cup and then smash the cup beneath their feet (on a tarp).

Table 7: The Wedding Supper — Revelation 19:6-9 and Revelation 3:20

This table is set up with chairs and elaborate place settings, plates, fruit, etc. It represents a great feast. Around this table are the words "He invites us to dine with him and be with him forever."

Worship and Prayer Station Interaction

After the message, people are invited to get up and walk through the seven tables in sequence. It takes about 30 minutes. People stop at each table to read the Scriptures, pray, read the words around the edge of the table, and interact in other ways set up for them at each table. People can also walk over to private prayer, journal, and art spaces. The band leads community worship from a stage in the rear of the room during this time. We show images and lyrics on the screens for the songs "Wonderful King," "Steadfast Love of the Lord," "Amazing Love" (hymn), "You Are So Good to Me," and "We Will Dance." The music begins very contemplatively, then builds toward the end.

Offering

Someone in the community prays for the offering and the bags are passed around as music plays in the background.

Closing Community Prayer and Benediction

A few minutes of open sharing are set aside for people to say short sentence prayers of thanksgiving out loud, especially about being the Bride of Christ. A prayer of benediction is offered after about three minutes. It commissions people for their mission to be the Bride of Christ throughout the week.

Walk-out Music

We play an ambient CD with no lyrics.

CHAPTER 14

Starting House Worship Church Gatherings

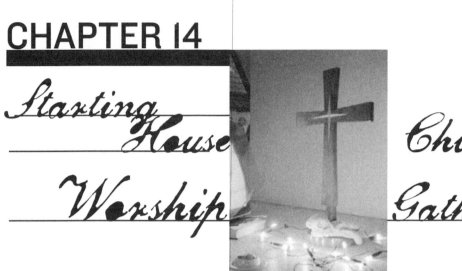

If we are talking about emerging worship gatherings, something we cannot ignore that is surfacing more and more in the emerging church conversation is the house church worship gathering.

When we say "house church," different pictures come to mind. So many different forms of house churches have existed throughout history that we cannot categorize and label them in a neat little pile. House churches are unique depending on their particular setting and leadership context.

As we read through the New Testament we will find that for a long time the church met together for worship in homes. House churches are the roots of Christian community worship.

In the Scriptures we read:

- "They broke bread in their homes and ate together with glad and sincere hearts, praising God…" (Acts 2:46-47).
- "…and so does the church that meets at their house" (1 Corinthians 16:19).
- "Give my greetings to the brothers at Laodicea, and to Nympha and the church in her house" (Colossians 4:15).
- "…and to the church that meets in your home" (Philemon 2).

As we begin to question why we do certain things we need to pay attention to the origins of our Christian worship practices. We will often find some startling similarities and contrasts between what "church" was to the early Christians and what we think it is — or long for it to be — today.

It wasn't until a few hundred years after Jesus Christ's ascension, for instance, that Christians moved from homes into church buildings. During the time of Constantine, churches grew much larger and adopted a much more formal order to what happened in the gatherings.

Emerging Generations Crave Something beyond "Small Groups"

Over and over again, I hear the rising dissatisfaction with what we typically call "small groups," particularly as a vehicle for worshiping together. There is a rising desire among emerging generations to be in smaller worshiping communities that are not so directly controlled as extensions of the larger church.

Emerging generations long to experience authentic community. They crave to be in a smaller worshiping community where they can have ownership, deeply share their lives (the good and bad), ask hard questions, and struggle with less than definite answers.

Some churches do have small groups where this happens. Where it doesn't, emerging generations are expressing increasing ripples of desire to move beyond the traditional form of small groups into a New Testament house church format as part of their worship experience.

House Churches Are Different than Small Groups

Churches may have small groups and home groups, but house churches function more independently and don't rely on a "mother church" to direct them. They function with their own leadership and make their own decisions. Everything isn't tied to a central church. Instead, you will find that most of the emerging house churches are networked with other house churches. This networking allows a sense of being part of the larger church community and also gives each of the house churches a sense of support and accountability to what happens in them.

For the purpose of this book I'm going to explore how house churches worship. This chapter by no means offers a comprehensive look at the way all house churches worship. I will focus most of my discussion on two examples of house church networks.

1. Why a new worship gathering was needed

Jason Evans was a full-time pastor at a contemporary church in southern California. It was a great job and he had the thrill of being given the task of starting a new worship gathering for emerging generations.

But things didn't work out as Jason expected. As soon as he started an emerging worship gathering at his church, he began to feel very unsettled. Although they provided lots of good music, good preaching, and incorporated multisensory elements in the new emerging worship gathering, he wondered whether this approach and focus for a church was really transforming people's lives.

Jason also wondered how much of what they were doing was simply transferring people from one church to another by means of the bigger and better programs and worship gatherings they offered.

Furthermore, he wondered why they were spending so much money on buildings, staff, and budgets every time he drove by migrant workers and homeless

"Worship the
LORD with
gladness;
come before
him with joyful
songs."
—Psalm 100:2

people living in cardboard shacks.

Eventually, this rethinking of what church is caused a crisis of conscience Jason could no longer live with. He quit his job and took another job working for a marketing company. He began to spend more time rethinking what "church" is supposed to be. Without any deliberate plan, he began running into other pastors who had similar experiences and had even left their churches. He also ran into other people, usually in their twenties, who had left megachurches and were seeking something different.

Jason had never even heard of a "house church." The only impressions he had were of militants and reclusive groups. But without even knowing they were forming a house church, Jason and the group of former pastors and other people who left their previous churches began meeting weekly in a home. They never formally started or planned to launch their house church. It just happened.

This group began meeting weekly to pray with one another and to explore what the Scriptures say the church is. They intentionally did not focus on what the church isn't. Their meeting was not a place where people came to grumble or criticize the church. Instead, they wanted to focus on what the church should be.

This small house church community sought to rediscover and re-imagine church from a fresh perspective. They would meet together weekly and worship together. Since that initial home church began, they have birthed other home churches as well. They now call this developing network of house churches Matthew's House.

A Young Adult Worship Gathering Turns into Another House Church Network

Axxess Fellowship began in an entirely different way than Matthew's House. Axxess began at Pantego Bible Church in Arlington, Texas. Pantego Bible Church is a thriving church with great preaching and wonderful contemporary worship gatherings.

Brad Cecil was part of Pantego Bible Church, but felt the restlessness that a new type of worship gathering was needed for our changing culture. So Pantego Bible Church asked Brad to help start "Axxess" as an additional Sunday evening worship gathering specifically designed for young adults. The plan called for Axxess to indefinitely remain a young adult worship gathering of Pantego Bible Church.

As time passed, however, Brad and others saw what was happening in the lives of younger adults and in our emerging culture. Axxess as a young adult worship gathering faced the very same questions that most young adult worship gatherings do: Is having a worship gathering with age limitations the right thing to do? Is this a generational issue or is this about something far greater than that? Is this more about a change in how we worship and think about church than a change in style of music and adding candles?

As time went on and they grappled with these questions, Brad and others eventually decided to became an all-age worship gathering at Pantego Bible Church that was designed for those with a more postmodern, post-Christian mindset. Time went on and they went through further transitions. Eventually, for philosophical reasons, they disconnected from Pantego Bible Church to become an independent church (with the blessing of Pantego Bible Church's leadership). But their transformation didn't stop there.

Axxess began rethinking even further about what church is. They wanted to live out being the church rather than going to church. They wanted to share life together as disciples of Jesus and not just go to a worship gathering. So they felt the best thing to do was to go though a rebirthing and turn Axxess into a network of small diverse faith communities who meet primarily in homes, apartments, and coffeehouses during the week.

Axxess moved from focusing on a weekly worship gathering with small groups to a network of house churches that meets to worship together in homes during the week.

For Axxess, a big reason they made this huge change was a question. They philosophically started asking, "How are people transformed?" not "What do we creatively do in an emerging worship gathering?"

Brad explains: "We believe that modernity promoted an idea that an individual is transformed through the exchange of information. Churches have bought into this idea and have built buildings to be large classrooms for didactic teaching, assuming that this is trans-formational. What if it is no longer transformational? We feel that transformation occurs as we share life. This is the ancient model of transformation and a very biblical model. So we have a very strategic reason for the move to the house church — this provides the optimal location for life exchange and therefore transformation."

The house church approach is not only about making a shift in methodology, it's about a shift in what the church is and how one approaches spiritual formation.

2. How the worship gathering functions in the whole church

With both Matthew's House and Axxess Fellowship, the question of how the worship gathering functions in the whole is an interesting one. The house churches don't see themselves as being attached to a single central church, since each of the house churches is a church. The way they function is more as a network of churches that retains a sense of the larger worship community.

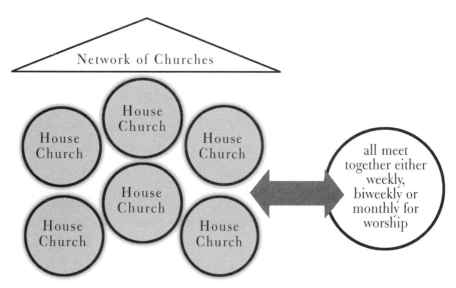

These networks of house churches meet weekly on their own as churches, but because they are networked they also meet together for worship in a larger context. Matthew's House churches meet once a month at a rented community center.

Originally Axxess churches met only once a month as a large group, but they sensed a desire to worship in community more often. So the house churches went back to meeting all together weekly on Sunday nights. They currently rent a church building for their weekly Sunday night gatherings.

3. How the leadership is structured in the whole church

Matthew's House is led by elders. The elders are the shepherds of each house church, and the elders of the house churches get together on a regular basis. The elders discuss how the churches are going and provide a time of encouragement and support to one another. The house churches themselves are pretty much self-led. There are no paid staff in Matthew's House as all those in leadership have other jobs. Each house church does have a name and is usually called by geographic location such as "Laguna Church," "Mar Vista Church," etc. There is offering taken in the house church meeting, and how it is spent is determined by the individual house church. It helps cover the meals that they eat together, and they use it to help the poor.

In Axxess Fellowship, a board of elders oversees the whole church. They don't have any paid staff at Axxess either. The elders are each part of various house churches. What Axxess does, however, is train and assign pastors to the house churches. They call them "pastors" since they are the ones who shepherd the house church. Becoming a "pastor" requires a lot of preparation and training. This way each house church has a specific spiritual leader who, along with the elders, watches and cares for the flock.

4. What does a house church worship gathering look like?

There are two worship gatherings that occur for house churches. The first is the weekly worship gathering that happens in the home. Each house church does things differently depending on the house church itself. Something that Jason Evans stated about house church worship gatherings is that everything they do is worship. There isn't a compartmentalization of worship beginning at a certain point. It is all worship.

The Smaller, Weekly Worship Gathering in Homes

In the Mar Vista Church of Matthew's House, a house church worship gathering starts with eating a meal together. They may take communion before the meal starts, or after the meal. The meal is the church breaking bread together (Acts 2:42). The meal is a time when people talk and are the church together. The beauty of a house church worship gathering is that there is no hiding. The atmosphere of love, acceptance, and worship allows people to really know one another and share life together.

They move to the living room after a meal and there is a lot of variety in what happens. When a worship gathering like this is not scripted or planned, the Spirit really can move a lot more in changing the direction of what occurs. But there still is order. *The Book of Common Prayer* is used for directed prayers and Scripture readings. There is some teaching, but it is only 10 or 15 minutes. The rest of the time is open discussion and interaction. They generally rotate the teaching and share it among those in the house church from week to week. They have some singing, but it is not the focus, and they may only sing a song or two. They have a time of meditation and may have a scriptural chant or prayer they say together.

The children in these gatherings are always together with everyone for the meal times. Depending on the house church, the children may stay in the worship meeting time itself, or in some house churches they separate. One house church in Matthew's House has a separate children's meeting after the meal where one person from the church each week rotates to teach and lead the children in a separate room while the parents meet. The meeting closes, and then they continue to hang out together.

In an Axxess Fellowship house church worship gathering, it is similar. One meets on Sunday morning and has breakfast together. People bring food and serve a buffet. They gather, talk over coffee, pray, eat, study Scripture, and pray some more. Children are welcome and sit with their parents unless they are too fussy, then parents can take them to a room with videos, books, and toys. In one Axxess home church, they have infants, toddlers, children, teenagers, college age, young adults, singles, marrieds, and older adults. They love the fact that it is mixed like this and not just one age group. This house church functions more like a family reunion each week.

The Larger Worship Gatherings for House Churches

With Matthew's House all the house churches meet together once a month. Before each monthly meeting, a group of elders and some in the house churches plan what that monthly meeting will be like. They meet in a rented community building, and they start off again with a potluck meal. They sing with a band, and they do a lot of what happens in the homes but in a larger setting. They report on how the various house churches are doing. They have some short teaching from one of the elders. They may have some silence, meditation, and take communion each week (people come forward to partake, rather than passing a tray down aisles). They may include some art pieces or create some things together. Children are part of the gathering so they can participate in the art worship.

In the Axxess Fellowship weekly gathering where all the house churches come together, they rent a church building on Sunday nights to meet in each week. The rough order of service is a greeting and invocation, then have a time of music as worship. They also take communion each week, and people can partake in communion at any time in the service when they are prepared to do so. They have a spoken word with some teaching, more worship through music, and end the gathering with a benediction/blessing.

The Axxess larger weekly gatherings are planned by the elder community and vary depending on what they desire to accomplish. One month the theme for their worship gathering was expressing worship to God through the arts. Throughout the month they invited several bands to lead an entire worship gathering. Filmmakers screened movies as an expression of worship. They expressed worship through artistic spoken words (slam poets, storytellers, etc.). They even chose to change the venue, using a coffee shop for the poets, a theater for the filmmakers, etc.

For the normal Axxess weekly worship gathering where all the house churches meet, the basic setup is a darkened, candlelit room, prayer rugs positioned throughout, Communion/Eucharist at the very center of the room is symbolic of Jesus Christ being the central focus. It is here where people can partake in the elements at anytime during the service; they move to the center of the room (sometimes kneel), partake, pray, and head back to their space. Children are welcome to stay in the worship gathering with their parents, but they also have a special class if they are not old enough to participate.

4. Summary and closing thoughts

I was extremely refreshed to listen to what is happening in these house church worship gatherings. Without a doubt there is an absolute sense of these churches viewing worship as something that occurs not only when they meet together, but all week long. There is no doubt of the church being the church and not being a meeting people attend. Quite honestly it really does feel extremely close to what the New Testament church must have been like. There is no sample worship gathering order for the house churches at the end of this chapter. They definitely have order and plan, but the meetings are so organic that a sheet with an order of the worship gathering is not necessary. I think you can get a feel from the description already written.

Spiritually Skinny-Dipping in House Church Worship

The sense of experiencing community as true community and not just forced-into-small-group-community is something I can only imagine as being where lives really are changed. But there is a cost to this type of community. Jason Evans described being in a house church worship gathering as "spiritual skinny-dipping" together. What he meant by that is that in house churches there isn't a whole lot of room to hide. In a larger worship gathering, people don't have to be in a small group. They can get by attending the larger worship gathering and sort of hiding. In a house church, you are in intense loving relationships, and that means exposure of who we really are and sharing of life together. This is a beautiful thing, but can be vulnerable and scary especially to those who have not experienced healthy relationships before. Not everyone is comfortable with this type of intimacy, although it is really what community is supposed to be about! We should be experiencing community like this, as it is in this type of worshiping community where spiritual formation occurs.

In these house church worship gatherings, in both smaller and larger settings we see the importance and value of having the whole family worshiping together. There are various ways this happens, as children's ministry occurs in separate meetings, as well as being all together. I also know of a house church that started teenage house churches to supplement the meetings the parents attend. The teenagers needed something especially for them, so they started almost what sounds like a mini-youth group in addition to the house church gathering.

Becoming Positive and Healthy Worshiping House Churches

I also think that these types of house church worship gatherings are so positive that they will break stereotypes of the ones that are more like refuge camps for bitter Christians that complain against the organized church. Also the fact that they are networked and not isolated can hopefully prevent some of the crazy things that can develop if house churches aren't somehow held accountable to someone outside the individual house church. There is a sense of leadership empowering that occurs here, too, as I can only imagine the sense of ownership and responsibility that having a "pastor" in each house church brings. It develops leaders in such a great way, rather than the usual, paid, seminary-trained "pastors" remaining the only ones seen as "pastors." Obviously, this means more training and maturity for the leaders of the house churches, but there weren't degrees and titles in the early church, either!

Is It Possible to Morph the House Church Approach with a Larger Church?

As I was thinking through all this, I wondered if it is possible to morph the values and philosophy of what house churches are doing in terms of worship, while still maintaining a centralized church. Is there a way to maintain the values and empowerment of a house church but also have the advantage of a centralized church?

Some of the house church worship approach is similar to some degree to what some emerging churches are doing, although they are not directly calling themselves a network of house churches. As described in the last chapter, Vintage Faith Church is building from a community of home groups/house churches, although we have a larger worship gathering. I know that we and many other churches are also teaching and trying to have the people *be* the church, versus *go* to church. Also, they're teaching that worship is not just when a meeting happens, but a lifestyle. I suppose time will tell as we all experiment together in this.

Emerging Worship in House Churches Sprouting Up All Around Us

Whether or not you agree with the house church philosophy, they are popping up all over. Emerging generations are being drawn more and more to a combination of house church gatherings with larger weekend worship gatherings.

In post-Christian England, St. Thomas' Church (www.stthomaschurch.org.uk) currently has about two thousand people, 70 percent of whom are under the age of 35. That is a huge number for a church in England, and we should pay attention to this. What attracts post-Christians in England is not to be ignored!

Here in America, Apostle's Church in Seattle (www.apostleschurch.org) is a new congregation whose people also are passionate about not just "going to a church," but being church in their daily lives and everyday interactions with other. They have a larger worship gathering that is very creative and multisensory, but they call their house church meetings "micro churches."

Apex Church in Las Vegas (www.apexchurch.org) also meets as a network of house churches.

More and more groups are experimenting with how house church worship can be the fabric of emerging churches. It's something that could be extremely important to our future. I certainly am optimistic that we can learn from the home-church movement. I believe it's possible, if leaders see it as important, to infuse larger churches with the values of house churches — many already are already moving into a "post-small groups" (as we know them) approach for building true community.

CHAPTER 15

Alternative worship in England  gatherings

They gave us the Rolling Stones, Sting and the Police, Led Zeppelin, Radiohead, Coldplay — and alternative multisensory worship that's now influencing emerging worship gatherings in the United States. I personally try to closely follow what the Holy Spirit is doing in England's churches because I believe that those growing up there outside of church circles (post-Christians, and now the majority) are very similar to emerging post-Christian generations here. They're listening to the same music, watching the same movies, and being shaped in their worldview much in the same way as those here growing up outside of Christian homes are. So, when post-Christian generations in England and Europe who grew up outside the church are resonating with worship there, we in America should pay attention.

Can't quite compare England and America

There are, however, differences between churches in England and America. England, for example, never had a seeker-sensitive church movement. Overall, the UK's Baby Boomers are the generation that left the church in the 1960s in much the same way as those born here after 1965 or so are abandoning the church now in the United States. Most churches in America have overcome the barriers of using drums, guitars, and bringing PowerPoint® into worship gatherings, and although they did also appear in British churches during the 1980s and 1990s, in most places such things were seen as pretty controversial and disruptive until very recently. Steve Collins, who lives in England and oversees an extensive Web site on alternative worship (www.alternativeworship.org), explains it like this. "In Britain we never had a seeker-sensitive Boomer church. Our churches here are just melting away, and the prevailing culture of churches remains a kind of a weakly modernized, traditional form of church. They're tired and old-fashioned. Our buildings are mostly 19th or 15th century. Forget the cinema seating in churches that you have [in America] now — we mostly have hard pews."

So, in terms of church methodology and the Christian subculture, there's a vast difference between American and British churches. And while the churches in England may seldom have embraced seeker and contemporary methodology, those who never experienced church there are similar to those haven't experienced church here yet.

In this chapter, we'll look at an alternative worship gathering in England called "Grace," which is part of St. Mary's Church in London, England. By looking at what they are doing (and why) in terms of worship, we may discover what resonates with post-Christian generations there.

1. Why a new worship gathering was needed at St. Mary's Church

In the Church of England has experienced a severe attendance decline since the 1980s. In fact, the English Church Attendance Survey from the year 2000 states that the number of young people in churches dropped by half over two decades. So a few Anglican churches began experimenting with new "alternative worship" services in existing churches. This wasn't simply a new outer dressing on what the existing church was doing to appeal to younger people; it was really an entire new paradigm of worship for the Church of England. Many youth workers began seeing their ministry in a missional context and moved to an incarnational approach in regard to their surrounding culture. So these worship gatherings began using popular culture in worship — but at the same time morphing it via historical, liturgical practices of the church.

These new worship gatherings occurred on Sunday nights or weekend nights and met in the mother church's building. As they attracted many new young people, they became known as "youth churches" or "youth congregations," but that didn't mean "youth" as we know it in America — it meant a mix of all ages, but primarily younger people.

The story of St. Mary's Church and the Grace alternative worship gathering is that a small group of young men and women decided to start a gathering that would be very different from the ones happening at their church. So, they began "Grace" as an alternative worship gathering that met once a month on a Saturday night and shared a community meal once a month on a Sunday night.

On the Grace Web site, they tell the story of why they started the new worship gathering: "Our major motivation at that stage had been dissatisfaction, an increasing frustration at church culture which played music we'd never listen to at home, used language we wouldn't use anywhere else and served up a diet which had become over-familiar and often irrelevant. Church had become something that was 'done to us', a dependency culture that we didn't fit into. But it wasn't all negative. We thought that there had to be many other people out there who felt like us, living in the pick'n'mix culture in which we were immersed. We didn't just want a room full of dissatisfied churchgoers, we wanted a worship gathering we could invite friends to."

2. How the worship gathering functions in the whole church

St. Mary's Church is Anglican and falls within the structure of Anglican leadership.

In turn, Grace is also considered a distinct congregation within St. Mary's Church. But Grace uses a different approach to worship in terms of style, theology, worship space, use of culture and technology, approach to leadership, and creativity. Some Grace attendees are part of other St. Mary's services; others attend Grace services exclusively. Either way, the desire of Grace is to build a worshiping community of its own.

Jonny Baker is a leader in Grace and explains how Grace and St. Mary's function together: "The strategy is not to see the people of Grace move to the main worship gatherings. Grace has its own cultural flavour. Why should people go to the other services? It's another world. It would be like the old, imperial mission stuff of expecting people to become Western in order to become Christian. So it wouldn't make sense to get people to cross over to the main part of the church and [embrace] a different way of doing things. But we do try and have relations with the wider church in other ways. For example, we will occasionally do a gathering for them or all get together at a social event.

"We have a very loose relationship with St. Mary's Church. We plan all our gatherings ourselves, not even running themes or titles past the vicar or leadership of the wider church. We occasionally meet to discuss how things are going, but it is relational rather than hierarchical. The vicar sometimes comes to the gatherings to worship and observe, or sometimes to preside at communion. But we are still very self-directed. In terms of missiology, we have what's known as the 'three-self principle' — self-administration, self-support, self-propagation. We don't have any paid staff, we are all volunteers, and we self-support Grace financially through our own offerings."

St. Mary's Church allowed a young group of people to birth a new worshiping community. We see that it's independent but still part of the whole church. Because the younger leaders were empowered to design and lead this worship gathering, it directly reflects how they wanted to express worship to God. They didn't have a particular form of worship imposed on them. We will see that instead of designing a worship gathering that was like others (but just with different music), they developed an entirely different worship experience.

3. How the leadership is structured in the whole church

Grace has its own leadership team of volunteers who meet regularly to plan their gatherings and other events throughout the week. Grace's relationship with St. Mary's isn't too formal. There isn't a reporting structure or formal meetings that take place on a regular basis. They also don't have a board or elders. Jonny Baker explains: "Anglican churches don't have elders. We currently do have a member on the church staff team — she's getting ordained this summer. She got involved with the church, as she wanted to get involved in Grace. But she is involved in Grace in the same way as every body else — it just gives us a better channel of communication with the wider church."

4. What a Grace worship gathering looks like

To really describe alternative worship as it's done in Grace, as well as in other alternative worship gatherings in England, words cannot do justice. They really are so visual, participatory, and multisensory that one needs images to describe them, not just words. On the Vintage Faith Web site (www.vintagefaith.com) we will be posting links to a lot of alternative worship Web sites, as well as providing photographs to see some of the things talked about in this chapter and about multisensory worship in general. You also can go to the Grace Web site (www.freshworship.org) to see visually what is being written about Grace, as well as (www.alternativeworship.org).

Seeking to worship God using their native language

To start describing what a Grace worship gathering is like, we should first look at some of the whys behind what they do. On the Grace Web site, they explain that "we seek to worship God in ways and forms that we can relate to, using the cultural resources of today which are our native language. This isn't a gimmick to try and reach young people. It stems from who we are and is an attempt to be authentic in that. This by no means excludes old things or even traditions, but the old things we incorporate (such as Celtic liturgy) are those that speak to our current situation, rather than hangovers from the past that remain through indifference or fear of change. Because we are feeling our way with things that are new, sometimes things don't work, but we accept that as part of what we are about."

Using the Senses and Rediscovering Contemplative Spirituality

"One aspect of the Christian tradition that we have rediscovered is contemplation. The overall feel of most services is fairly contemplative, and we usually incorporate some sort of meditation. We try and incorporate ritual, discussion, and liturgy that engages people rather than that which is passively consumed. Using the body and senses is important — we try to get away from the over-cerebral nature of most church services. Sometimes it's necessary to be, not just to think."

You can immediately tell that Grace sees its meetings as moving away from preaching as a form of communication and worship bands singing songs. Alternative worship gatherings like Grace actually are different than most of the emerging worship gatherings in America, even the more progressive ones. There are similar patterns, as there is the inclusion of prayer stations that people can go to, participatory stations to be contemplative and quiet, etc. But in America most emerging worship gatherings still have some sort of teaching and some corporate singing. In the alternative worship gatherings in England, worship becomes more of an experience or environment through which you make your way, gently guided by the directions of the team and the design of the worship space. Teaching isn't up-front and verbal because it's been built into everything that happens, so people can discover things for themselves. Beginnings and endings are informal — in effect, they are "announcements" that the event is open or has finished.

There may be some communal readings of a prayer, but it's typical to say at the beginning that people don't have to take part in anything if they don't want to. It's usual to say at the end that people are welcome to stay longer. The event becomes a worship experience that one walks into and stays as long as one wants to. It's not sequential or rigid;

it's fluid and nonlinear. The gatherings start when one enters the room. There is ambient, chill-out, meditative music playing in the background. You would be greeted and then directed to what is happening that night.

Different Themes Throughout the Church Calendar Year

The worship space is set up differently according to the theme of the night. Grace chooses specific themes that they design their creative worship gathering around. Depending on the theme, various spaces and stations are created that you walk through and stop at. At some of these stations you participate and write something or create something. At others you just stop and pray.

Jonny Baker explains it like this: "There isn't one typical format to a Grace worship gathering. Each one is different, and for the theme of the worship gathering, we tend to tie in with a theme from the church calendar. The last service was a Stations of the Cross service. We took the traditional Stations of the Cross — 14 stopping points on Jesus' journey to the cross—and our leaders took on different stations so there was a shared responsibility. We then set up the stopping points as stations/installations around the church meeting room. We had a café going as well, so this way when people came, they could walk through the journey of the 14 stations as they liked. The whole thing ran for 4 hours, and people could come and go as they pleased. It was for all ages — we encouraged people to bring their kids to walk through the stations, too."

One of the stations was a computer screen on a stand, draped in black cloth. The screen showed Scripture and images so that participants could stop to read and also respond by praying and writing prayers in a journal left at the station. You could move from there to another station that consisted of a large cross, and you would actually make a cross from materials and then nail it to the bigger one. There was a station with a rock slab on the ground inscribed with the words "I AM the stone that makes them stumble," representing where Jesus fell for the first time. There was a station where you would stop and paint.

There was a station where you would leave imprints of your hand in sand. Each of these stations provided written direction regarding its spiritual metaphor or symbolic meaning in relation to the Stations of the Cross. There were also Scriptures for people to read and stop and meditate upon. There was also a station where people went outside to place a stone on an old tomb symbolizing the tomb of Christ.

This is merely a thumbnail description of what one of these gatherings is like, but as you can tell it is filled with Scripture, with experience of the senses, and with prayer. These alternative worship gatherings are community experiences — ones that draw many to worship God and listen for his voice. They may sound very foreign to what a traditional worship gathering is like, but that's because these churches are rebirthing what a traditional worship gathering is like for their context so they can relate to the way people living around them desire to express worship and prayer.

Something interesting that Steve Collins points out is that in England they don't use too many ancient symbols in these worship gatherings. "In British alternative worship there is some hunger for the ancient stuff — meaning pre-reformation/catholic/orthodox — that was off the map or forbidden fruit to most of us. But we also had an enormous hunger for the truly, brutally new. It's a postmodern 'new' — chaotic, unreasonable, maybe confrontational, not the calm let's-all-agree rationality of modernity that occurs in worship. It's about engaging with the world right now — with its language, its media — rather than escaping into the comfortable past as churches so often do. You can see it in things like typography and imagery used in worship. To me as a designer, it's really striking how emerging churches in the United States have 'churchy' styling — gothic and medievalizing. This is exactly what English emerging churches are trying to escape from! Compare the Web sites of American and English emerging churches. This is because most of our churches lack technology beyond overhead projectors and microphones, so creating a technological environment with laptops, TVs, and electronic music is a powerful gesture in our context. It says 'Christianity can be expressed through 21st century life and isn't stuck in the past — that's a big deal here, because people see Christianity as 'over,' having nothing left to say."

5. Summary and some thoughts

I can't begin to count how many hours I have spent on various alternative worship Web sites from England. They have inspired me to think about worship differently and to rethink what we do in our worship gatherings. When I first found out about what was happening over there, it felt like they had put into action some of the very things I was feeling about worship, but hadn't yet figured out what to do with what I was feeling. It was an extremely refreshing and stimulating thing to discover what was happening in England and how they brought to flesh many of the instinctual feelings that a lot of people are having here in the United States about worship gatherings.

Asking why alternative worship is resonating with emerging generations

As we said earlier in the chapter, we cannot simply copy what is happening there and implant it here in the same way. I lived in London for a year, so I have some understanding of the culture there compared to the United States. But what we can do is pay attention and ask why these alternative expressions of worship are resonating with post-Christian generations in England. I very much believe that post-Christian generations here will also resonate with similar forms of worship. (By post-Christian I'm referring to those who grew up outside the church and therefore have not yet been tainted too much by a church experience.) Both British and American post-Christians share in common a culturally implanted worldview that differs from the traditional Judeo-Christian worldview.

Regarding alternative worship gatherings, we should ask why post-Christian generations are resonating with this type of worship. I know that it is the Spirit who draws us to Jesus, and worship is not something one puts together like an activity to participate in; but what can we learn from these alternative worship gatherings in England? We see their desire to slow down and be contemplative in addition to the typical upbeat rhythms and upbeat songs. In these alternative worship gatherings there is ambient, meditative music playing and the understanding that people can take their time and pray, read Scripture, etc.

Some singing may occur, but singing is not the focus of worship.

In our emerging worship gatherings, perhaps we need to designate times for silence, for slowing down, for prayer at length. To experience joy and praise, but also to allow people to quiet their hearts and be contemplative.

We also see how alternative worship gatherings in England use creatively designed prayer stations where people can stop to interact and respond in worship. This is something we also can be adding to our worship gatherings. We may want to take note that teaching can occur through other means than a sermon. In alternative worship the experience itself "teaches," the prayer stations and Scriptures teach. Even if we still keep preaching and teaching in our gatherings, we can add other forms of teaching and recognize them as valid and effective.

Worship expressed in the way emerging generations desire to express it

Probably the most exciting thing we can learn is that Grace's worship of God is worship that they themselves shape. They're free to design their worship expression in a way they feel is best for who they are. I hope that we will empower emerging generations to design worship gatherings as well instead of leaving that only to paid staff.

I hope we can be asking God if anything from England's alternative worship services can be incorporated into our local contexts. Most alternative worship gatherings in England are not too large, so there may be creative thought used to bring elements of worship into larger gatherings. But the important thing is that alternative worship reflects the specific community expressing worship in a way that shows worship is not just what happens at a meeting, but something people do all the time in their lives. The Grace Web site explains, "For most of us, this process involves making church out of the elements of our everyday lives — the issues, the culture, the language, the media, the music. Church becomes more like home — a place where we belong and which belongs to us. And this can help us to see that home, and the rest of our world, can be church — life lived in the presence of God."

Sample Worship Gathering

Grace at St. Mary's Anglican Church, Ealing, London

Theme: The Emmaus Road

8 p.m. Saturday

Worship environment

The event takes place in two large rooms that open fully into one other. One is set up as a café from which people arrive and depart. The other contains the worship stations.

In the café the lighting levels are low, and each table has three candles. Refreshments include wine, soft drinks, and snacks such as pretzels or nachos, cakes, and anything else the team brings. There's no charge, but there is a plate for donations.

The worship space is fully visible to people in the café. The room appears warm and intimate, softly lit from the stations and TVs. There are small candles everywhere. The stations are around the edges of the room; the center has a carpet and cushions around a tall, central candle. Ambient video loops are running on old TVs stacked in corners and incorporated in the stations, sometimes on their sides or upside down. The video content is appropriate to the service theme but is there to create atmosphere and reinforce messages rather than be given full attention.

Background music is playing in both rooms, from a CD mixer or an iPod plugged into the sound system. The music is relaxing, largely instrumental, electronica flavoured with jazz and funk as opposed to rock. It creates a warm, sociable yet slightly mysterious atmosphere, and is not loud enough to inhibit conversation. Music will play continuously all evening behind everything that happens, with lowered volume or quieter tracks when people are speaking. The sound system is just inside the worship space but off to one side so that the DJ is part of what happens but not the focus. For much of the time the DJ leaves the equipment to run itself while taking part in the worship.

Opening

On arrival people are welcomed by team members and invited to wait in the café for the formal beginning of the service. When enough people are present, one of the team members welcomes them to Grace and gives a short introduction to the theme of the evening. Another member of the team then reads the story of the meeting on the Road to Emmaus, Luke 24:13-35.

The worshipers are then invited to visit the stations at their leisure, but not all at once so as to avoid overcrowding. They are told they will have an hour or so to go through the stations, which removes "deadline" pressures from those who wish to think and pray in the worship room or socialize in the café. The feel of the gathering is friendly and informal throughout, but more quiet and prayerful in the worship space. The team mixes with the rest of the worshippers at all times except when speaking or facilitating.

The stations

Each station has the relevant Bible verses as well as the other things described. Many stations have additional material not recorded in the order of service. Team members are responsible for their own stations and can elaborate or change as they wish within the theme. Much of the final form and content is as new to other members of the planning team as it is to regular participants.

On this occasion the stations have a sequence as follows:

Station 1: The hiddenness of God [Luke 24: 13-16]

This station is about the "dark night of the soul," and how the experience of the absence of God can be legitimate and not the result of sin. There are "magic eye/stereogram" books conveying the idea that God may be present, but we do not see. There is also the story of the dwarves who cannot see Aslan's kingdom (from *The Last Battle* by C.S. Lewis).

Station 2: Downcast [Luke 24: 17-18]

This station contains the "bitter herbs" from the Passover meal. Worshipers are invited to taste these and read Psalm 22.

Station 3: Storytelling [Luke 24: 19-27] part 1

The disciples on the road to Emmaus were consoling one another by telling stories and remembering Christ. Worshipers are invited to write about a time in their life when they met with God, leaving their stories to be read by those who follow. The station consists of a polling booth fortuitously left in the church that week so people can write on their cards in the booth and pin them up on it.

Station 4: Storytelling [Luke 24: 19-27] part 2

About the power of hearing God's story, how this strengthens us in dark times. In a second polling booth is a CD player with headphones. The music is "Jesus' Blood Never Failed Me Yet" by Gavin Briers.

Station 5: Welcoming the stranger [Luke 24: 28-29]

Who is the stranger for you today? Have you ever encountered Christ in or through a stranger? The worshiper is invited to contemplate 10 photographs of different kinds of people.

Station 6: Breaking bread [Luke 24: 30-31]

A loaf of bread on a table, flanked by candles and an open art book showing Caravaggio's painting of the moment when Christ breaks the bread and is recognized by the two disciples. The picture is also projected on the wall behind the station. There is a meditation about recognizing Christ; there are many copies of this to take away. Worshipers break and eat pieces of the bread.

Station 7: Burning hearts and telling others [Luke 24: 32-35]

How are you going to tell others about Christ? How will you express your faith to others? There is a short piece of writing to think upon, and worshippers are invited to light candles and pray for others.

As well as following the "road," people sit or lie in the center of the room to pray, write, or think. Others are still in the cafe or have returned there.

Ending

After about an hour, when everyone who wishes has followed the "road," we gather again in the cafe. A team member leads us in a short liturgy that she has written for this evening. It brings together the ideas and messages of the evening before God with prayer and congregational responses.

After this formal ending, people can stay to eat, drink, and talk for another half hour or so before the team starts to take down. Often people stay longer to help. Any who wish then go to a nearby Indian restaurant for a late meal.

CHAPTER 16

Is Emerging Worship Simply Creating a Generation new of Christian Consumers?

If any man builds on this foundation using gold, silver, costly stones, wood, hay or straw, his work will be shown for what it is, because the Day will bring it to light.
— 1 Corinthians 3:12

I once spoke at a conference on multisensory worship. A group of eager pastors and church leaders watched my PowerPoint® slides of prayer stations built for people to paint and creatively express themselves in worship. I spoke about the use of looping videos and shared creative ways to set up a room to be more interactive. While I enthusiastically spoke about these things, in walked someone I hadn't seen for a while. It was a missionary who had just arrived from northern Iraq and Nepal (yes, we are all missionaries wherever we are, but he is a missionary overseas).

This person travels a lot. His missionary newsletters talk about the incredibly horrific scenes of hunger, starvation, and AIDS in the various countries he visits. He has been to some of the most difficult and dangerous countries in terms of their hostility to the Christian faith. In these places, being a believer in Jesus can cost someone his or her life.

This missionary probably doesn't have much money. He is the type of person who would spend his last 20 dollars to feed and help poor people. Especially since 20 dollars in other countries can go a long way and sometimes save the life of someone who is starving.

Because all the chairs in the room were taken, he slumped down on the floor and sat crosslegged against the wall. We caught each other's eye; he smiled and waved. And then I began to feel very miserable and uncomfortable.

Multisensory Worship in Light of Starvation, AIDS, and Persecution

Here this missionary sat on the floor, having seen starvation, AIDS, homeless people, and persecuted Christians who could be killed if their smuggled Bibles were found. Here he sat knowing Christians in certain countries who desperately search for secret places to meet and worship together without being caught and arrested.

And here I was. Talking about nifty ways to float candles in man-made ponds. Talking about how to use video-projectors that cost several thousand dollars. I felt sick inside as I struggled through the remainder of my workshop.

I was so horribly conscious of all my words. I felt so incredibly consumeristic, shallow, and even ridiculous when compared to the desperation others in the world face. When I finished speaking, I awkwardly packed up to go. Then my missionary friend walked over. We said hello and a few quick words to reconnect.

Before we went much further, I blurted out, "I feel so stupid talking about all this with you here!" I apologetically explained how petty I felt talking about emerging worship gatherings and addressing things such as room design, art, and prayer stations.

Being Missional in Different Cultural Contexts

He smiled as he listened. Then he gently put his hand on my shoulder and said, "Hey, you are doing what is needed here in much the same way I have to do things differently where I go. We're both being missional in different cultural contexts." He went on to tell me how he knows that in America, multisensory forms of worship are forms that resonate with those who have grown up in this culture. He shared how growing up in a certain culture affects how people express worship.

Then he said something that relieved me greatly. He said that he always looks forward to coming home because his church in America does a lot of things with multisensory worship. He told me he loves worshiping God in his church using the very same multisensory approaches I had talked about.

We took a walk together. As we walked, he affirmed me and told me to not feel bad because he agreed with all I had said. We talked about worship being more than just what happens in a worship gathering. That was something of concern to him, as well.

By having forms of worship that use the arts and creative expressions, do we teach people that is all there is to worship? Is worship just the experience, or is worship the sacrifice of praise and offering all we are to God? We discussed this great danger in the church. Whether traditional or contemporary, modern or emerging, we as leaders have the responsibility to teach what worship really is.

A church may use multisensory worship and expensive video projectors to connect to the culture and communicate about Jesus and Kingdom living. If it ends there, however, it becomes sin. It becomes narcissistic. It creates another generation of Christian consumers who consume the worship experiences their church provides.

That is where the emerging church must be different! We will be utterly ashamed at the judgment seat of Christ if we put on great multisensory worship gatherings and teach people that consuming worship is Christianity.

"The 24 elders fall down before him who sits on the throne, and worship him who lives for ever and ever. They lay their crowns before the throne and say: 'You are worthy, our Lord and God, to receive glory and honor and power, for you created all things, and by your will they were created and have their being.'"
—Revelation 4:10-11

Sacrificial Worshipers vs. Consumer Worshipers

In the excitement of emerging worship gatherings, we need to be careful not to subtly train people to become consumers of worship. Rather, they must be worshipers who are living selfless, sacrificial lives and thinking of others more than themselves. Worship is not about us. It is about sacrificing our lives for God and serving others. It's about recognizing who God is and standing, kneeling, and singing out our praises and adoration to him. This means that as a result of the Holy Spirit at work in our worship gatherings, we should be seeing the people who are part of them loving God more and loving people more. Loving others means to put others needs above our own. So this raises some questions.

In addition to the money we spend to facilitate our worship gatherings, how much money do we spend on the poor and needy? How much money do we spend on overseas missions where an American dollar goes such a long way? For the price of a new video projector, we could save the lives of dozens of children who are starving.

How much time and energy goes into setting up artwork, prayer stations, and candles in a room compared with the time spent sending people into inner city areas to help urban churches? How much time goes into serving the elderly in our communities? How much time goes into sending people overseas to needy areas to build homes and help in orphanages?

Woe to us if we use nifty things to create worship experiences for emerging generations but ignore and forget those Jesus told us not to ignore. Jesus' answer to the question in Matthew 25:44-45 should be remembered with great soberness as we lead our emerging churches: "They also will answer, 'Lord, when did we see you hungry or thirsty or a stranger or needing clothes or sick or in prison, and did not help you?' He will reply, 'I tell you the truth, whatever you did not do for one of the least of these, you did not do for me.'"

Emerging Worship should Produce Sacrificial Worshipers

You see, the ultimate goal of creating and designing emerging worship gatherings is to glorify God and make disciples; it's not about the cool things we do in worship. Yes, we should fully think through designing and creating multisensory worship gatherings. But that is not the goal. The goal is to see those in our church community become disciples of Jesus and sacrificial worshipers.

A disciple is someone about whom Jesus says, "If anyone would come after me, he must deny himself and take up his cross daily and follow me. For whoever wants to save his life will lose it, but whoever loses his life for me will save it" (Luke 9:23-24).

Jesus didn't say, "If anyone would come after me, he must use multisensory worship through videos and candles and art stations."

One Day We Will Give an Account

We have a serious responsibility in all of this. We in leadership have a critical role in shaping what the people in our churches think a follower of Jesus looks like. We have a holy responsibility to decide how money is spent as an act of worship. We better not ever spend money frivolously on art supplies, videos, or candles without seeking God. It is essential to ensure that what we do with the resources he has provided is what he wants, and is in balance. I believe that designing very creative worship expressions and all the things we talked about in this book are healthy and beneficial things. However, we must never lose perspective.

We need to be on our knees, asking God to show us how much time and energy to spend on the worship gathering and how much time and energy to spend on other aspects of spiritual formation for those in our churches. We need to be on our knees asking God how much time and energy we should encourage people in our churches to put into coordinating worship gatherings versus helping the poor.

We best never forget that one day those who teach will be judged more strictly than others (James 3:1). We teach people not only from the pulpit, but from where we place values in our churches. We teach people how to spend their time. We teach people what is important by how we spend money that comes in our offerings. This is pretty serious!

We are also told in the Scriptures that those who shepherd the church "keep watch over you [the church body] as men who must give an account" (Hebrews 13:17). One day we will give an account for how we led the people whom God entrusted to us.

The Ultimate Question We Must Answer

It is a serious thing for those who lead the church to keep a sober and prayerful watch on the balance in their ministry. We must prayerfully steward our time and resources in a way that pleases the One we serve. We must constantly ask the ultimate question, "Do the emerging worship gatherings we create produce disciples or consumers?"

We will give account for this ultimate question. Not whether we used all five senses to worship or whether we prayed with ancient creeds. If we do not ask the most important question about making disciples in emerging worship, we run the risk of building with wood, hay, and straw (1 Corinthians 3:12).

It is a holy privilege to be involved in leadership in Jesus Christ's Church. I pray that more of us will rise up to the challenge of rethinking church and worship for our culture. I pray that we will teach those who are part of our emerging worship gatherings to love not worship but the One we worship.

I pray that we will work hard to create and express innovative worship, but not at the expense of losing our first love in Jesus (Revelation 2:4). I pray that after a worship gathering, we will lie in bed at night, not thinking about the creative art and prayer stations we set up, but thinking about the people we saw kneel in worship and prayer at the stations.

I pray that we will not celebrate the numbers in our worship gatherings.

Instead, let's celebrate the people who serve and bring the Kingdom to others as a result of being in our worship gatherings.

I pray that in our communities we will not be known simply as churches of creativity and innovation. Instead, may the emerging church be known as a worshiping church, a serving and selfless church, a holy church, and a church of love and grace.

May God bless you on the journey of leading new generations in emerging worship.

"All of history is moving toward one great goal, the white-hot worship of God and his Son among all the peoples of the earth."
—John Piper

Cover Image Descriptions

Upper right image: Magi Star

One of the prayer stations at an outdoor labyrinth called "A Christmas Journey" that was created in the carpark of Opawa Baptist Church in New Zealand. A creative representation of the star that the Magi followed to find Jesus, it was part of a series of stations that retold the Christmas story. (Photo by Cobra.)

Center top image: Angels announcing the birth of Jesus

A photo of the prayer station that focused on the angelic announcement of the birth of Christ to the shepherds. (Photo by Cobra.)

Center middle image: "Alienation" prayer station

A prayer station where people make a cross with twigs and ribbon as they pray for those who suffer from alienation. (From Resonance, at the Greenbelt Festival, England; photo by Steve Collins.)

Center lower image: Prayer Labyrinth

A prayer path is marked on the floor, and people walk the path slowly, are given Scriptures to read, and participate in various interactive prayer experiences. Communion is served in the center. (Photo by Steve Collins.)

Interior Photo Credits

Joyce Majendie (pp. 1, 63, 141, 209)
Steve Collins (pp. ix, 25, 39, 49, 99, 115, 127, 167, 195, 225)
Cobra (pp. 13, 73, 155)

Appendix of Emerging Worship Resources

An Emerging Church and Emerging Worship Web Site

www.vintagefaith.com

On www.vintagefaith.com we will continue the conversation started in this book and in my previous book, *The Emerging Church*.

Online there are two additional chapters you can read:

A Personal Plea to Senior Pastors
A Personal Plea to Emerging Leaders

On the vintagefaith.com Web site are sign-ups for a free monthly e-zine highlighting further content Web-only content:

- Links to other emerging worship Web sites, blogs, and art
- Articles and interviews about emerging worship
- Photo archive of emerging alternative worship gatherings in the United States
- Ideas from different churches regarding alternative worship

Emerging Worship in the U.S.

If you have photographs and ideas regarding emerging worship gatherings in America that you want to contribute to the www.vintagefaith.com Web site archive, please e-mail us. We look forward to developing a source that connects people with ideas, photos, and examples of emerging worship gatherings from all across the country.
—Dan Kimball
dan@vintagefaith.com

Emerging Worship Web Sites from the UK

www.alternativeworship.org
www.emergingchurch.info

These Web sites provide insight and examples regarding what is happening in the UK alternative worship movement.

Labyrinth Online

http://web.ukonline.co.uk/paradigm

In emerging worship gatherings, the prayer stations mentioned in this book are similar to the stations of multisensory labyrinths recently created. You can experience an online labyrinth on the above Web site. During the online labyrinth, you can pray and worship – it may even spark ideas for prayer stations that you may want to create in your local context.

Other Helpful Web Sites

www.emergentvillage.org	A friendship of missional Christians
www.emergentys.com	Resources and books for the emerging church
www.theooze.com	Articles and a bulletin board about culture and church
www.next-wave.org	Articles about emerging culture and church
www.jordoncooper.com	A blog keeping tabs on culture and the emerging church
www.allenon.net	Thinking through what "church" is
www.ginkworld.net	Articles and interviews about church and culture
www.sacramentis.com	Sally Morgenthaler's Web site of articles and links

Churches Featured in This Book

As you browse these and other emerging church Web sites, always look beyond the worship gathering. What else is each community doing to make disciples and cultivate true spiritual formation?

Westwinds Church	www.westwinds.org
Axis at Willowcreek Community Church	www.generationaxis.com
Frontline at McLean Bible Church	www.frontline.to
The Gathering at McLean Bible Church	www.generationalmovement.org
Genesis at Twin Lakes Church	www.tlc.org
Vintage Faith Church	www.vintagechurch.org
Santa Cruz Bible Church	www.santacruzbibe.org
Matthew's House	www.matthewshouse.com
Axxess Fellowship	www.axxess.org
St. Thomas' Church	www.stthomaschurch.org.uk
Apostle's Church	www.apostleschurch.org
Apex Church	www.apexchurch.org
Grace at St. Mary's Church	www.freshworship.org

Other Emerging Worship Web Sites

www.smallfire.org and www.alternativeworship.org
You can lose yourself for hours on end with these two Web sites. They feature articles and photographs of the alternative worship movement in England and other parts of the world. Steve Collins, with whom I dialogued to create the www.vintagefaith.com interactive bonus chapter on "Exploring Alternative Worship Gatherings in the UK," is the one behind these Web sites.

www.sacramentis.com
Sally Morgenthaler's Web site about worship has tons of links to art, articles, and other emerging worship resources.

Helpful Books

Ideas for Emerging Worship

The Emerging Church: Vintage Christianity for New Generations by Dan Kimball (Zondervan, 2003). My first book discusses deconstructing postmodern ministry and reconstructing vintage Christianity in the emerging church.

Alternative Worship: Essential Tools for the Emerging Church by Jonny Baker, Doug Gay, and Jenny Brown (Baker Book House, 2004). This book explores alternative worship gatherings in England. One of the authors, Jonny Baker, is part of Grace at St. Mary's Church.

Soul Shaper by Tony Jones (Youth Specialties, 2003). This book looks at the ancient spiritual disciplines and gives suggestions on how to implement them today.

The Book of Uncommon Prayer: Contemplative and Celebratory Prayers and Worship Services for Youth Ministry by Steve Case (Youth Specialties, 2002). This book gives specific examples of a variety of worship practices.

2,000 Years of Prayer by Michael Counsell (Morehouse Publishing, 2002). This book contains hundreds of prayers written throughout church history.

The Book of Common Prayer (Oxford University Press, 1979). This book features prayers and community readings and responses tied into the seasons of the Christian calendar year.

The Divine Hours by Phyllis Tickle (Doubleday). The three books (so far) in the Divine Hours series features prayers compiled from the Bible, *The Book of Common Prayer*, the early church fathers, and other sources.

Celtic Prayers From Iona by J. Phillip Newall (Paulist Press, 1997) This short book contains Celtic prayers from the Iona community.

Worship and Church History

A Brief History of Christian Worship by James F. White (Abingdon Press, 1993). This book divides the history of worship into eras and looks at what each era did regarding church architecture, preaching, communion, and more.

The Wonder of Worship: Why We Worship the Way We Do by Keith Drury (Weslyan Publishing, 2002). This book traces the origins of what we do in church worship services.

Protestant Worship: Traditions in Transition by James F. White (John Knox Press, 1989). This book takes a fascinating look at worship from the Reformation to today.

The Biblical Foundations of Christian Worship by Robert E. Webber, editor (Hendrickson, 1995). This book looks at worship practices throughout biblical history.

Worship Old and New by Robert Webber (Zondervan, 1994). This book looks at worship through the lenses of history and theology.

Pagan Christianity: The Origins of Our Modern Church Practices by Frank Viola (Present Testimony Ministry, 2003). I disagree with many of the conclusions and the tone of this book. Still, this book offers a detailed history of many modern worship practices.

Holistic Approaches to Worship Gatherings

Church Re-Imagined: The Spiritual Formation of People in Communities of Faith by Doug Pagitt (Zondervan, 2004). This book focuses on a holistic look at a missional church and shows how the worship gathering fits within the whole picture.

The Missional Church: A Vision for the Sending of the Church in North America by Darrell Guder, editor (Eerdmans, 1998). This book will shape your thinking about how a worship gathering fits into a church's purpose and mission. I highly recommend chapters 4 and 5.

The Divine Conspiracy: Rediscovering Our Hidden Life in God by Dallas Willard (Harper Collins, 1998). This is probably the most influential book I have read about spiritual formation and holistic church ministry.

The Arts and Worship

God Through the Looking Glass: Glimpses from the Arts by William and Aida Spencer (Baker, 1998). This book takes a biblical look at why and how art, dance, sculpture, film, and drama can be integrated into faith and worship.

Visual Faith: Art, Theology, and Worship in Dialogue by William A. Dyrness (Baker House, 2001). This book takes a theological look at why art is an important part of how God communicated to us and how we can incorporate art into our worship of him.

A Journey into Christian Art by Helen De Borchgrave (Fortress Press, 1999). This book is a great resource for reading about the history of the development of Christian art. It's also a source of images to use for worship gatherings.

The Doré Bible Illustrations (Dover Publishing, 1974). My favorite artist of biblical scenes is Gustave Doré. His artwork powerfully illustrates many scenes from the Old and New Testaments.

House Churches

The Church Comes Home: Building Community and Mission through Home Churches by Robert and Julia Banks (Hendrickson, 1998). This is a very practical book about how house churches can function. It also presents theological and biblical reasons why they should be considered.

House Church Networks: A Church for a New Generation by Larry Kreider (House to House Press, 2002). This book is an introduction to house church networks and builds a case for why emerging generations resonate with this approach.

Paul's Idea of Community by Robert Banks (Hendrickson, 1994). This book focuses on what community looked like in New Testament times and how home worship gatherings were a vital part of that era.

Other Resources

Worship Image Gallery on CD-ROM: 700 Photos & Digital Artwork for Visual Churches (Zondervan). This CD-ROM contains great images for using as backgrounds for song lyrics, Scripture quotations, and other writings projected during emerging worship gatherings.

Prayer Path: A Christ-Centered Labyrinth Experience (Group Publishing). This kit provides most of the materials and instructions to create your own labyrinth. This labyrinth was an inspiration for a lot of ideas we have used in our prayer stations.

Highway Video (www.highwayvideo.com). Highway Video offers a variety of videos and other visual and sound elements specifically designed for emerging worship gatherings.